Penguin Education

Penguin Science of Be
*General Editor:* B. M. Foss

**Cognitive Psychology**
*Editors:* P. C. Dodwell and Anne Treisman

**Listening and Attention**
Neville Moray

Penguin Science of Behaviour
*General Editor:* B. M. Foss

Professor of Psychology, Bedford College,
University of London

Abnormal and Clinical
Psychology
*Editors:* Max Hamilton
Nuffield Professor of Psychiatry,
University of Leeds
Graham A. Foulds
University Department of
Psychiatry, Royal Edinburgh
Hospital

Cognitive Psychology
*Editors:* P. C. Dodwell
Professor of Psychology,
Queen's University at
Hamilton, Ontario
Anne Treisman
Institute of Experimental
Psychology, University of
Oxford

Developmental Psychology
*Editor:* B. M. Foss
Professor of Psychology,
Bedford College,
University of London

Industrial and Organizational
Psychology
*Editor:* Peter B. Warr
Deputy Director of the
Medical Research Council
Social and Applied Psychology
Unit, University of Sheffield

Method and History
*Editor:* W. M. O'Neil
Deputy Vice-Chancellor,
University of Sydney

Motivation and Emotion
*Editors:* Dalbir Bindra
Professor of Psychology,
McGill University, Montreal
Jane Stewart
Associate Professor of
Psychology, Sir George
Williams University, Montreal

Physiological Psychology
*Editor:* K. H. Pribram
Research Professor of
Psychology and Psychiatry,
Stanford University

Skills and Learning
*Editor:* Harry Kay
Professor of Psychology,
University of Sheffield

Social Psychology
*Editor:* Michael Argyle
Institute of Experimental
Psychology, University of
Oxford

Neville Moray

# Listening and Attention

Penguin Books

Penguin Books Ltd, Harmondsworth,
Middlesex, England
Penguin Books Inc., 7110 Ambassador Road,
Baltimore, Md 21207, U.S.A.
Penguin Books Australia Ltd, Ringwood,
Victoria, Australia

First published 1969
Reprinted 1972
Copyright © Neville Moray, 1969

Made and printed in Great Britain by
C. Nicholls & Company Ltd
Set in Linotype Times

This book is sold subject to the condition that
it shall not, by way of trade or otherwise, be lent,
re-sold, hired out, or otherwise circulated without
the publisher's prior consent in any form of
binding or cover other than that in which it is
published and without a similar condition
including this condition being imposed on the
subsequent purchaser

# Penguin Science of Behaviour

This book is part of an ambitious project, the *Penguin Science of Behaviour,* which covers a very wide range of psychological inquiry. Many of the short 'unit' texts are on central teaching topics; while others deal with present theoretical and empirical work which the Editors consider to be important new contributions to psychology. We have kept in mind both the teaching divisions of psychology and also the needs of psychologists at work. For readers working with children, for example, some of the units in the field of Development Psychology will deal with techniques in testing children, other units will deal with work on cognitive growth. For academic psychologists, there will be units in well-established areas such as Learning and Perception, but also units which do not fall neatly under any one heading, or which are thought of as 'applied', but which nevertheless are highly relevant to psychology as a whole.

The project is published in short units for two main reasons. Firstly, a large range of short texts at inexpensive prices gives the teacher a flexibility in planning his course and recommending texts for it. Secondly, the pace at which important new work is published requires the project to be adaptable. Our plan allows a unit to be revised or a fresh unit to be added with maximum speed and minimal cost to the reader₃

Above all, for students, the different viewpoints of many authors, sometimes overlapping, sometimes in contradiction, and the range of topics Editors have selected will reveal the complexity and diversity which exist beyond the necessarily conventional headings of an introductory course.

B.M.F.

For my stepfather
John L. Higson
with gratitude

# Contents

# Editorial Foreword

This book is the first to appear in a series which will explore different aspects of attention. Attention is an elusive concept to define objectively. For this reason psychologists deliberately neglected it in the earlier decades of this century, often at the cost of making their theories of behaviour less plausible. However, in the past twenty years, research into attention has gained new impetus, and fresh ground is now being broken in many different areas. Fields to which the concept is relevant range from the physiological study of how animals orient to novel stimuli to the performance of air-traffic control tower operators. This new series, of which Moray's book is the first, will throw light on a wide range of different problems relating to attention and in so doing will, I hope, bring into relief some common underlying brain mechanisms.

Perhaps the most effective stimulus to the recent revival of interest was Broadbent's work on selective listening, which he began in the early 1950s. This was important both in its practical implications and in the intellectual excitement aroused by his 'filter theory' of attention, which showed how one could investigate and explain attention by means other than the fallible and unreliable methods of introspection. In *Listening and Attention* Neville Moray explores Broadbent's research and its fruitful ramifications. Although, after reading this interesting survey, one may feel, as he does, that new problems have been raised as quickly as old ones solved, I think this is a sign of research that is alive and progressing.

Dr Moray is well qualified to review this area since he has himself made important contributions to it. Active involvement in a problem often leads to controversy with others similarly engaged. In this book Moray presents not just a textbook of facts, but his personal view of the current status of a lively and growing area of research.

A.T.

# Preface

The study of attention has intensified greatly during the last decade. This book is concerned with one small area of it, namely the ability of man to listen to one of two or more messages. It includes work on control-tower style communication systems, on speech shadowing, on attention switching, on auditory psychophysics, on physiological studies of selective listening and on the so-called 'split-span' memory experiment. As far as possible I have tried to keep closely to the topic of selective listening. Thus I have not discussed the split-span experiment in detail, since it seems most likely that its interpretation has more to do with the properties of the memory system than with auditory selectivity, and short-term memory will be dealt with by another author in this series. In the same way I have omitted much of the physiological work on the properties of the reticular system, since, while it is undoubtedly concerned with the general topic of the mechanism of attention, it seems to have little to do explicitly with selective listening.

Criticisms of several current theories will be found, mainly destructive. I do not underestimate the heuristic value of such theories, but a critical appraisal of the field strongly suggests that we know far too little yet to attempt to construct theories of the complexity which has been seen in recent papers. All current theories are probably wrong, and none of them has really been adequately described by its proponent (for example, Treisman gives no account of how switching occurs, Broadbent does not specify the time constants of the filter, etc.). The book then is a report of work in progress, and as such I offer it to the reader.

I would like to express my gratitude to several people who have helped explicitly or implicitly in the production of this book. Anne Treisman and Donald Broadbent have provided stimulating criticism and help during the ten years in which I have been engaged on attention research, and have contributed a very great deal to our knowledge of attention. I would also like to thank the staff and students of the Sheffield Department of Psychology who have discussed my ideas and helped with experiments. The manuscript was first prepared during a sabbatical leave at the Massachusetts Institute of Technology, and my thanks are due to Professor H.-L. Teuber and Professor W. Rosenblith for making my visit there possible; and to the Fulbright Commission who paid my travel. Finally, I would like to thank my wife for help with the proofs; and the editor of the series, Anne Treisman, for her helpful discussions and willingness to print passages in which I may have misrepresented her theoretical position, and about which we could not agree.

# 1 Perception and Communication: The Starting Point

A newcomer to the field of selective listening is fortunate in having a single source of information by means of which, although his knowledge is incomplete, he may regard himself as *au fait* with most of the facts that he needs to know about work up to 1958, with the exception of auditory psychophysics. That source is the now classical review by Broadbent (1958), *Perception and Communication*. It covers a field far wider than selective listening, but includes a very extensive review of work in the area which interests us; while the model that was proposed by Broadbent, the 'Filter Theory', has generated most of the subsequent work, and has been extremely important in restoring work on 'attention' to its rightful place in experimental psychology. Most ideas which occur to those working in selective listening today can be found foreshadowed in Broadbent's book.

The experiments which make up the bulk of early modern work in selective listening were performed in the context of applied problems, and tried to provide answers to a particular set of problems which are of increasing importance because of the tendency of modern society toward reduced physical effort and the massive increase in the rate of transmission of information that forms the basis on which human beings interact with their environment. Although the most popular name for the field is 'the cocktail party problem', namely how to listen to one voice when many are speaking at the same time, there are much more important implications. As man spends increasing amounts of time interacting with machines, or with other men through the intermediary of machines, and as the amount of communication and control in the world increases, it becomes increasingly apparent that the weakest link in the flow of data and commands is man. In particular there are situations where men find themselves confronted by several verbal messages arriving simultaneously or at least densely packed into a short space of time, and where it is vital that the messages be separated out and each receive an appropriate reply. One example of this is the air-traffic control tower, where several messages may arrive from different aircraft within a very short space of time. And, of course, it would not do to underestimate the social importance of correctly hearing what is said to you at a crowded party (crowded, that is, as a communications channel, regardless of the number of individuals present!).

## The Question and Answer Method

Most of the early experiments were of the 'question and answer' type. Listeners heard one or more messages, and after the messages had ended were required to repeat them, identify them, or answer them. They thus differed considerably from the series of experiments to be discussed in a later section, where speech is listened to continuously, and monitored for some change to which an immediate response is required, with the memory component of the task minimized. However, it appears that despite this difference there are a number of generalizations which have been derived from the question and answer experiments that can be applied throughout the experimental work on selective listening, regardless of the methodology employed.

Of these generalizations, the first is one which is intuitively obvious. The more that two messages resemble one another in every respect, the less will they be separable; and conversely, the more likely it is that the listener will treat them as a single message. The most extreme case of such close resemblance occurs, of course, in the ordinary binaural reception of messages. In this case the input to the two ears is from the same voice; at the same loudness except for minor effects of headshadow and has the same pitch and content. The only differences will be produced by headshadow, asymmetries of non-linear distortions produced by the external and middle ears, and the fact that with sound travelling at a rate of approximately thirty centimetres per millisecond there may be a delay of up to some few hundred microseconds in the time of arrival of the sound at the two cochleas. These differences are insufficient for the inputs to be treated by the nervous system as distinct messages, and a single, fused, coherent message is heard, the differences in the times of arrival being interpreted as differences in the localization of the sound source in auditory space.

The dimensions which have been most exhaustively studied as possible bases for auditory selectivity are loudness, pitch, position in auditory space, and message continuity (meaning and syntax). Egan *et al.* (1954) thoroughly investigated the effects of extreme source separation on the dimension of auditory localization, the effect of filtering out certain frequency regions, and loudness differences, in a 'question and answer' type of experiment. The task was to detect the presence of a message and to identify the words of which it was composed. *Dichotic* presentation (when one message is presented to one ear, another to the other) was shown to be markedly superior to *monaural* presentation (where both messages were presented to the same ear), and the improvement was equivalent to increasing the signal to noise ratio of the selected message by up to 30 dB compared with the monaural case (see Figure 1). Filtering the messages also improved the intelligibility of the selected message, whether it was the accepted or rejected message which was filtered. When the two messages began simultaneously, were presented monaurally, and were spoken by one speaker at the same intensity, then the articulation score (a measure of the accuracy with which the messages could be identified) was 50 per cent. When the accepted message was high-pass filtered the articulation score rose to about 70 per cent; while if the rejected message were high-pass filtered, the articulation score of the accepted message rose to over 90 per cent. The message to be identified was in each case preceded by a call sign ('Langley Base', 'Mitchellfield').

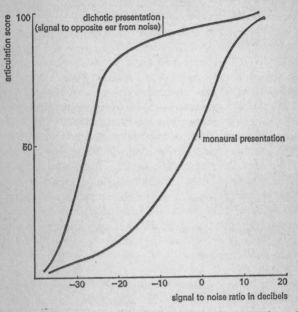

Figure 1 Advantage of dichotic over monaural presentation using masked speech (after Egan *et al.*)

The cue value of loudness as such, regardless of which message was the louder, appeared when messages were presented which were alike in all respects except for their verbal content and loudness. As the selected message was made less and less intense, while the intensity of the rejected message was held constant, the articulation score of the selected message fell at a rate of about 4 per cent per dB of the signal to noise ratio. There was, however, one exception. When the accepted message was very slightly softer than the rejected message, in the region between 0 dB difference (equally loud) to —10 dB, the articulation score did not change. So it appears that in this region the increasing distinctiveness of the selected message, the fact that it was slightly quieter than the rejected message, more than compensated for the increased masking of that message by the rejected message which must have been occurring. Presumably it provided a cue which allowed the listener to determine which words belonged to that message. Once the difference in loudness was more unfavourable still to the selected message the articulation score fell rapidly. It is interesting to note that Tolhurst and Peters (1956) found that if two messages were presented binaurally with no instructions as to which was to be selected the probability of the correct repetition of a message was simply and directly a function of the relative loudness. The louder message was always the better reported. If we compare this result with that of Egan *et al.* it provides clear evidence that voluntary attention, the determination on the part of the listener to select one message at the expense of the other, does in fact make a difference. Selective attention is a psychological reality, not merely a subjective impression on the part of the listener.

Problems of Definition

This is a good point at which to introduce a problem to which we shall have to return later, the problem of the operational definition of 'attention' or 'selectivity'. It has been observed by several writers in recent years that there was a great deal of research on attention up to about 1910, but remarkably little thereafter until the 1950s. The laboratories of Wundt, Titchener, Pillsbury, writers such as Hamilton and James all dealt extensively with the nature of attention. (Bakan, 1967, provides a good source of readings for this early work.) But after those workers attention research fell into disrepute, until restored to renewed respectability through the work of Broadbent in particular in the mid-fifties. One reason for this marked break in the continuity of research is without doubt that the early definitions of attention were tied rather too closely to the common intuitive idea that paying attention to a stimulus makes it somehow 'perceptually clearer'. Consequently the main method of investigation was introspection, with all the well-known problems of method and standardization which that implies. Even the more direct experimental approaches of Titchener are remarkably hard to replicate. The rise of behaviourism led to great difficulties for those anxious to justify attention as a respectable topic for research, since in many ways it was almost a paradigm of a 'mental' faculty. Behaviourism therefore lumped it with other mentalistic constructs as things to be avoided by all right-minded scientists, and since then the pursuit of an appropriate operational definition has been arduous and long. For example, it is only very recently, with some of the models proposed by Sutherland (1964) and Mackintosh (1964) for animal learning and shape discrimination that anyone has found a way of incorporating something akin to attention in a theory of animal behaviour in any except the most vague and general way.

One trouble is that the everyday uses of the word 'attention' are so many and varied. It is prone to the fate which Gibson (1941) so long ago pointed out as having overtaken the word 'set', which at the time that he wrote already had more than a dozen different meanings in the literature. Too many meanings, without sufficient precision in their use, without adequate operational definition, leads to a concept becoming less valuable the more promiscuously it is employed. This present monograph is concerned with attention in the sense of *selection,* and especially with selective listening : but the final chapter will offer some suggestions for a more general taxonomy of attention tasks. For the present it is sufficient to note that we might want to say of the experiment by Tolhurst and Peters that the listener's attention is 'caught' by the louder message, whereas in Egan *et al.*'s experiment attention can voluntarily be directed to the quieter of the two messages. Such a claim implies that we think that as experimenters we can distinguish between the masking of the quieter message by the louder message, and the use of the cue of greater loudness as a means of selection. Only the latter ability is relevant to the question of the nature of selective mechanisms as such. Egan's results show that all the interference is not masking: some of it may be overcome, and that 'part' is due to distraction, not masking. In general it seems that the distinction between involuntarily having one's attention caught and voluntarily paying attention is both important and meaningful.

Following this line we must examine the role which the call signs play in such experiments. There is ample evidence (Broadbent, 1952, 1958) that prefacing a message with a call sign makes a great deal of difference to the ability of a listener to select one from two or more messages. It seems that the greatest difficulty that a listener experiences in selecting a message is identifying which is the message he is trying to select. A call sign gives the listener an opportunity to gain information about the characteristics of the voice which carries the message (where it is, what are its pitch and loudness, its timbre, and so on) before the critical part of the message begins which contains the non-redundant content. Presumably selection is then made on the basis of these characteristics.

## Dimensions of Selection

To what, then, does a listener selecting a message listen? To everything arriving through the chosen ear? To signals of a certain pitch? Or, a possibility having quite different implications for the way in which the selective mechanisms are organized, does he actually listen to the verbal content of the message itself, which happens to have the characteristics (such as its pitch) which he has used to identify it? Consider the dichotic case again.

It seems intuitively plausible (although almost certainly it is false) that when a listener is asked to select one of a pair of dichotic messages he might 'turn off' an ear if localization is to be the basis of selection. He would then receive the message through the 'open' ear. On the other hand, he might carry out the same instructions not by turning off an ear but by using the first few words to establish the content and syntax of the message arriving through the designated ear, which would be identifiable by its position (left or right) in auditory space, after which he would select his input on the basis of the transitional probability between the signals, listening to the *message in* the ear rather than *to* the ear itself.

The importance of message continuity as a basis of selection is seen in an experiment by Cherry (1953). He made up two messages for binaural presentation, which were composed of strings of political clichés extracted from Hansard. Listeners who heard the two simultaneously presented cliché strings were asked to report what they heard. Despite the severe masking of each by the other, listeners could with practice separate the messages. But while they accurately reported the content of the message within a cliché, they tended to cross from one message to another at the cliché boundaries. Clearly the lack of high transitional probabilities between the last word of one cliché and the first word of the next made selection impossible while the presence of such cues within the cliché helped the listener to attend to it. It is possible, therefore, that the physical properties of the voice, and the content of the message which it speaks may provide independent methods of selecting auditory messages, and one would expect very different neural mechanisms to be involved.

Much of the work on selectivity has used dichotic presentation. This is really an extreme form of auditory lateralization or localization. But unlike messages which arrive from the auditory world of every day life, messages which are localized 180° apart do not stimulate both ears. Providing that the intensity level of dichotically presented messages is sufficiently low to avoid bone-conducted cross-talk between the ears (this takes place at about 70 dB re $0 \cdot 0002$ dynes cm $^{-2}$ according to Zwislocki, 1953), each message only stimulates one ear when dichotically presented. Looking at such experiments it is very easy to fall into the trap of thinking in terms of 'turning off' one ear when constructing hypothetical models. Such temptations should be strenuously resisted. In the real 'cocktail party problem' both ears receive both messages, and yet selection can be carried out. Indeed, it is comparatively rarely that a listener finds himself in a position where two competing sound sources are completely localized to the left and right. (About the only one which occurs to the writer is that of a girl being simultaneously courted at the party by rival suitors each hissing blandishments in their respective ear.) Rather, one must think of selection occurring with respect to the internal representation of auditory space inside the brain, a space of many dimensions from which some region may be selected as that from which a message is acceptable.

There is at present no good theory of how this should be described. It might be, for example, that messages are re-routed through neural circuits which represent different parts of this space; but it could be that instead each message is transmitted along with a 'tag' which assigns a number to the message describing where it was located, and that in selection no re-routing actually occurs. However, while dichotic presentation is not frequently encountered in real life, conclusions from such experiments can be generalized. Thus Spieth *et al.* (1954) found that spatially separating loudspeakers by quite small amounts helped the selection of messages from a specified loudspeaker. Treisman (1964b) found that in a shadowing experiment some 20° separation was sufficient to prevent words being imported from the wrong message, although there was still some interference even when the messages were separated by as much as 90°. Moray *et al.* (1965) found that a listener seated in the middle of an array of four loudspeakers could select one of them and show almost perfect performance when told in advance which one to use. The loudspeakers were separated by 90°, and the messages were short lists of random letters, up to four items

per loudspeaker, which the listener had to recall at the end
of the presentation. They also found that there was no difference when split headphones and lateralization were used,
compared with the localization of four loudspeakers.

To revert to the point made earlier, we know that listeners
can select one of two messages to shadow if they are spoken
by speakers of different sexes. Thus a listener can select a
male and ignore a female voice when they are presented
monaurally (Treisman, 1964b) for shadowing. Clearly this
is a case where selection is not synonymous with turning off
an ear. Indeed in this case the basis of selectivity is rather
slight, since a spectral analysis of the frequencies present in
the voices of male and female speakers shows only slight
differences. Apart from the fundamental pitch, almost all
the frequencies are in common, and one must bear in mind
that the higher frequencies carry most of the non-redundant
information in a speech wave. All these results should make
us very sceptical of physiological evidence which seems to
imply the turning off of an auditory input. Selection is within the internal space whose dimensions are pitch, loudness,
location, time of arrival, etc., and it is for a mechanism which
would operate on such a space that we must search.

It may well be that the ability to make use of the content
of a message rather than its physical characteristics depends
on timing to a large extent. Spieth *et al*. (1954) found that if
the message to be selected begins more than 0·2 seconds
before the rejected one, then it is more likely to be correctly
perceived than if the asynchrony is less than that amount.
Time relations of a rather different order of magnitude,
probably involving memory mechanisms to a considerable
extent, were also evident in an experiment by Broadbent
(1958). Investigating the effects of overlapping and inter-
leaving messages with both messages needing to be reported,
he found that even when the messages taken signal by signal
did not overlap there could be very bad interference between
them. Sentences of the form 'Is is the my cat aunt on in the
the mat garden?' showed very poor performance even

though there is no masking of one message by the other.

Except for the last mentioned experiment, most of the work cited has been concerned with cases where one message was to be reported and another to be rejected. It is not necessarily true that conditions which aid a listener to make that kind of a response will help him if he must respond to more than one message. Broadbent (1954) found that increasing the spatial separation between loudspeakers did not improve performance invariably if both the messages had to be monitored. One might also expect that when the only distinguishing feature apart from content is the loudness of the two messages, widely differing separation along the loudness dimension would hinder the reception of both, since as we have seen outside the range of relative loudness 0 to 10 dB, the louder message will progressively mask the softer.

## Speech Shadowing Experiments

Similar and closely related results have come from the long series of experiments using speech shadowing which have appeared during the early 1960s. The technique was introduced by Cherry (1953) and consists in asking a listener to repeat a continuous prose message while he receives it. It has been called 'verbal tracking' by one or two workers, which well describes the relation between the stimulus and the response. The duration of the message may be varied from a few words to several minutes of continuous prose, and the task is really a degraded form of simultaneous translation, in which the message is translated into itself. Most of the experiments have used presentation rates of about 150 words per minute, which with a bit of practice can be attained easily by most listeners. No work has been done on very highly practised listeners; and it should perhaps be mentioned that experimenters who have worked for a considerable time on shadowing often find that they cannot readily test the recordings they have made for synchrony, since their own shadowing ability improves to such an extent that their performance is no longer subject to the limits of beginners. This needs investigating.

Cherry's original observation was that when a listener shadows a message presented to one ear while ignoring a different message presented to the opposite ear, he can afterwards say of the rejected message only such things as whether or not it was speech, whether a man or woman's voice, etc., but can not report any of its content, or what language it was spoken in. The results have frequently been summarized by saying that all that is available from the rejected message are the 'simple physical characteristics' (see Figure 2).

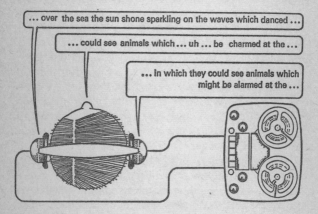

Figure 2 The speech shadowing experiment

The great popularity of the technique stems from the extraordinary way in which shadowing seems to lock the listener on to the required message. It offers a way in which the experimenter can guarantee that the listener is paying attention to the indicated message to a degree that is difficult to achieve in any other kind of experiment. Moreover, any wandering of the attention from the selected message is instantly detectable in the reduction of the efficiency with which the listener repeats the accepted message. It is not yet wholly clear why the technique is so very effective. Moray (1969) has suggested that it may be merely a very easy way of keeping the listener so busy that he has no time to sample any other message. The first experiment to take up Cherry's lead found that his original claims were substantially correct. Moray (1959) found that if the rejected message consisted of a set of seven words repeated thirty-five times during the shadowing of the accepted message, no trace of retention for the list could be found using a recognition test administered twenty seconds after the end of shadowing. Recently this result has been confirmed by Norman (1969a) but with the additional observation that if the delay before testing is reduced to not more than a second there is good evidence of retention, at least of the material which was presented in the rejected message immediately prior to the moment of recall. Apparently the content of the rejected message disappears within a second or two, which suggests either that it is not stored in the usual short-term memory store, or that it is stored in a very degraded form. We shall refer to this question again shortly. Mowbray (1964) found that if shadowers were given the additional task of recalling short lists of numbers from the rejected message if they should occur, they could only do so at the cost of a very marked failure in shadowing around the point where the numbers occurred in the rejected message. Subjectively, most listeners agree that they are not aware of the content of the rejected message.

Subsequent research has made the picture considerably more complicated, and it has begun to appear in the last year or two as though our models will have to be extensively revised. In general it is easy to reproduce Cherry's findings. But detailed examination shows that at least some information is in fact affecting the listener when it is presented in the rejected message, although the listener may be unaware normally of what is happening.

Moray (1959) inserted instructions to change ears, or to

stop shadowing into the messages, embedding them in prose. The instructions were heard in the accepted message, but not in the rejected message. However, if the instruction was prefixed by the listener's own name, it was heard on about 30 per cent of the trials. He also (Moray, 1969) was able to make a neutral word 'significant' in this way by pairing it with electric shock. Despite the listener not hearing the word when it was presented in the rejected message, conditioned GSRs to its occurrence were obtained. These results should be considered along with the experiments by Howarth and Ellis (1961) and Oswald *et al.* (1960) which also show the privileged position of a listener's name in the hierarchy of auditory signals. The former measured the detectability of one's own versus other people's names when masked by white noise, and found that the threshold for one's own was lower. The latter presented lists of names to sleeping listeners, while recording the EEG. They observed that sleepers woke more frequently to their own than to other names, gave more K-complexes in the EEG (a measure of arousal) to their own than to other names, and gave more GSRs to their own than to other names. In the case of the last two indices the result was observed even when the sleeper did not awake. Howarth and Ellis present an ingenious argument to suggest that the three experiments are all tapping the same mechanism. Taken together they suggest that information even of non-attended signals arrives at high levels of the brain, probably at the cortex, and that selection is not a peripheral mechanism. (There is, for example, good evidence that the cortex is needed in man for the establishment of conditioned GSRs to complex patterns, and that discrimination of complex patterns such as occurred in Oswald *et al.*'s experiment would also require the cortex.)

Treisman (1964b) provides conclusive evidence against the selective mechanism being in the extremely peripheral parts of the afferent pathway. She presented one message to the left ear, one to the right ear, and one to both ears. The lateralization effect resulted in their being heard respectively at the left ear, the right ear, and in the midline, inside the head. She could then ask her listeners to shadow the middle message, which they could do. It is clear that one does not turn off both ears in order to listen to the central message (see Figure 3).

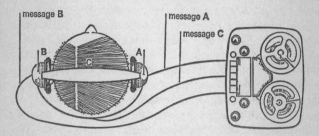

Figure 3 Three-channel listening: use of loudness differences to achieve lateralization of sound images

When message C is equally loud in the two ears, it is heard lateralized in the midline, inside the head

We began this section with the generalization that the more similar two messages are the less efficiently one may be selected and the other rejected. The question of similarity has been investigated by Cherry (1953), Moray (1960, unpublished), and most extensively by Treisman (1964c). All three studies produced the same results. Suppose that we present a prose message to a listener's right ear and ask him to shadow it. To the left ear we present the same message, but leading or lagging in time. How far apart must the two messages be in order for them to count functionally 'different' as far as the selection mechanisms are concerned?

To some extent it depends on what type of material is used as a stimulus message. Coherent prose must have a greater separation than a string of random digits. But if the listener is shadowing the leading message, so that the rejected ear receives the message after the listener has heard and repeated it, then the separation at which they are recognized as being the same is surprisingly large. All three workers found that most listeners spontaneously noticed the identity of the messages when they were at least five seconds apart, and some of Treisman's subjects noticed the identity at more than eight seconds. An obvious interpretation of this would be that there is a trace left in a short-term memory by the reception of the selected message, and that this trace is matched with the input from both ears. Eventually it either fades spontaneously or is erased by the subsequent selected input, and so disappears. But for several seconds a sufficiently high correlation between the trace and the rejected message will result in the nervous system treating the two messages as identical, with a resulting breakdown of attention. The two messages do not fuse into a single image: rather, an echo-like effect is produced. But at least it is impossible to keep the two separate. (The maximum delay at which two dichotic inputs will be heard as fused into a single, coherent message is of the order of twenty milliseconds.)

Notice that it is not necessary to assume that the meaning of the two messages is being compared. It would be sufficient given the evidence which we have, merely to correlate the overall wave envelope of the two messages. We shall see later a case where such an assumption is inadequate to explain a similar effect.

The results are quite different when it is the lagging message which is shadowed so that the material which the listener accepts has already been presented to the rejected ear at an earlier moment. Now the messages have to be brought within a second or so of one another before selection fails. If the accepted message lags by more than this, it is functionally a different message from the rejected message. What is the reason for this striking difference?

The crucial separation is a matter both of the time and the number of words. At the rates of speech usually used, the leading difference is over twelve words, and the lagging about two. Now it could be that the reason for the difference is that the rejected message is not stored, or does not enter the nervous system at all. Hence there is no trace left by it to be compared with the same material when it later arrives over the accepted channel. But we have seen that there is ample reason to think that at least some representation of the rejected message does in fact enter the nervous system. It is noteworthy that when shadowing the lagging message the critical separation is very close to the maximum time for which Norman found retention of rejected material. But rather than postulating a quite different memory store, we might suggest that the rejected message is in fact stored in a rather degraded form, 'attenuated' as Treisman would say (see below, p. 36), and therefore the trace lasts only for a second or so before it is too noisy to be used for successful matching with the accepted message. We do not know whether the breakdown occurs at some particular point in the message; whether it is the onsets of the words which are crucial, whether some words are more likely to lead to recognition than others, and so on. Detailed investigation of these questions might lead to valuable insights into the way in which the material of the rejected message is used.

Treisman has also investigated the role of meaning, loudness, and voice quality in selection (Treisman, 1964a and b, 1960). She found that listeners can shadow a voice of one sex and ignore that of the opposite sex when monaural presentation is used, and that similarly loudness can be used as the basis of selection. In the earlier paper, she presented messages dichotically and asked listeners to shadow the right ear. Half way through the message the two messages exchanged sides, so that the message which had been on the left was now on the right and vice versa. At the moment of changeover, listeners typically repeated one or two words from what was now the wrong ear, and then reverted to the original ear and continued to shadow the 'new' accepted message. They were unaware of having switched. Clearly in this case the high transitional probabilities between successive words from a prose message were crucial in making the

listener switch messages, but the voluntary setting of attention then over-rode the passive switching and restored the
setting of the selective mechanisms to their original state.
This brings out very clearly the distinction mentioned earlier between selecting an ear and selecting a message in that
ear, and between passive and active attention.

One of the most interesting findings of Treisman concerns
the role played by language in the control of attention. The
reader will recall that Cherry found that shadowers could
not report the language in which the rejected message was
presented. This is in general true. Treisman (1964a) investigated the role of language using binaural presentation. She
presented an English prose message and a translation into
French of the same message binaurally. She then compared
the performance of groups of subjects who had different degrees of fluency in French. Truly bilingual subjects produced
responses which included mixed French and English phra-
ses, showed a great deal of interference, and frequently could
not separate the two messages. This suggests that for messages which are spatially close the identity of the selected
and rejected messages can be detected even when the sound
waveforms are totally dissimilar. The words, phonemes even,
of English and French are very different; but because the
meaning as such, independent of the speech waveform which
carried it, was the same, the messages were treated as identical by the brain. The message must then reach the level of
the nervous system where meaning as such is extracted. She
also found, however, that with dichotic presentation there
was very little interaction between two messages one of
which was a translation of the other.

The curious fact seems to be that while the listener is usually unaware of the more complex features of the rejected
message, it is just those, rather than the simple physical
characteristics of the waveform, which cause attention to
switch. Moray (1958), for example, found that merely making the rejected message louder than the accepted message
made little difference to the shadowing performance, at least

as measured by omissions and commissions in shadowing. When the rejected message was 10 dB louder than the accepted message the interference began to increase, although there were very few importations from the wrong message, and at the levels of presentation which he was using there may well have been some bone-conducted cross-talk at that intensity, which would begin to produce peripheral masking. The content of messages seems to be used by the selection mechanisms, but is frequently not accessible to consciousness. To foreshadow a theory which will be proposed later, notice that this might be for two reasons. Firstly, the 'strength' of the rejected message might be weakened to a level where it cannot be consciously recognized. On the other hand, it might be that the strength of the message is not reduced, but only very short samples of it are allowed through to the analysing mechanisms, with the same result.

One important point to note about all the above results is the absolute frequency with which the effects occur. While it is true that people tend to hear their own names, they did so in Moray's experiment, only on about 30 per cent of the trials, and in general that is an upper limit. There seems to be no report in the literature where attention was involuntarily switched on more than 33 per cent of the trials, and in most cases, such as Treisman (1960), the frequency of occurrence of switching is very much less. This is very important in understanding how information 'leaks' through from the rejected message, since it implies that a given stimulus will not always cause attention to switch, even though it may sometimes do so.

With the above results in mind, let us look at some of the theories which have been proposed to account for them.

# 2 Theories of Selective Listening

Several reviews of attention have appeared recently, but only three contain well-formulated theories. Several do little more than systematize the experimental results, sometimes including work from fields other than hearing (see, for example, Egeth, 1967; Reynolds, 1964). But the three models which have received most discussion have been those of Broadbent (1958), Treisman (1960) and Deutsch and Deutsch (1963). In addition a compendious review of closely related work is provided in the stimulating book by Neisser (1967) including a model related to 'analysis by synthesis' which does not seem to the present writer to be very helpful with regard to selective listening, but is very provocative in other ways. Norman (1968) has recently elaborated further the approach of Deutsch and has incorporated memory in it. Moray (1969) has tried to summarize all the major auditory and visual work up to 1968, paying particular attention to methodological problems and experiments using non-verbal stimuli.

## Broadbent's Filter Theory

The first modern model for attention was the now classical Filter Theory proposed by Broadbent in *Perception and Communication* in 1958. This proposes that the human operator is a limited-capacity information channel in the sense of information developed by Shannon (Shannon and Weaver, 1949). The peripheral nervous system obviously comprises a number of different input channels (vision, hearing, somaesthesis) each of which has many parallel input lines. At some point in the nervous system, it is argued, there is a bottleneck in the flow of information, since the central channel has a lower capacity than the combined capacity of the peripheral receptors and neural input lines. Notice that a limited-capacity channel can carry information in parallel providing the maximum capacity of the channel is not exceeded, but even so, with the massive amount of information arriving at the body's surface, the central processor is frequently overloaded. When this happens, Broadbent proposes, the only way in which the system can handle the situation is to sample sequentially the various input channels, much as a uniselector samples its various contacts, except that the order in which they are sampled can be varied, and the fraction of them which are sampled at all is variable. Such sampling converts parallel input to serial transmission, thus keeping the latter within the bounds of the central processing channel. Broadbent proposes that there is a short-term memory store at the end of the input lines, so that when two messages arrive simultaneously one of them is transmitted instantly, while the other is held in store until the line is free. During its time in store the representation of the message fades, due to autonomous decay and interference from other material that arrives, so that by the time it is handled it will be degraded. Presumably it is not necessary for it to be handled at all if total rejection of that message is the aim of the listener.

The crucial experiment on which the model is founded is the 'split-span' experiment which we shall discuss below, but the model covers a much wider field than selective listening or even attention in general. The selection mechanism is the switch which determines the input channel to be sampled, and various special properties are hypothesized for the channels. For example, on the basis of empirical studies Broadbent proposes that the probability that a certain channel will be sampled when it eventually contains a signal increases with the length of time which has passed since the last time that it was sampled. The 'channels' were originally thought of as being fairly closely identified with sensory pathways, but this can no longer be accepted, since, as we have seen, language or voice quality can be used as criteria for selection, and later we shall see that verbal classes can likewise be used. Broadbent mentioned the latter possibility, but with the filter acting on peripheral inputs it is hard to see how it could be implemented, since the members of verbal classes have meaning, rather than phonemes or frequency components, in common. It is doubtful how far the original model can be modified to deal with these facts, although we may note for a start that there is some ambiguity in the meaning of 'channel'. In information theory the channel would not be the hardware of the brain, but the set of signals passed through it by the nerve impulses, modulation of which carries the 'information'. The information which can be carried by a telephone line is limited by the bandwidth of the signals used to transmit the message, and only indirectly by the hardware organization. The cable is limiting only in so far as it limits the bandwidth. Once one realizes that the channel is not, strictly speaking, the nerve, but the set of signals it carries, the idea of selecting a 'channel' which is a language is less implausible, involving the selection of patterns rather than transmission lines. Broadbent's system would, however, also run into difficulties over the partial breakthrough of information from rejected messages if, as he originally stated, the time taken to sample and switch was of the order of 750 ms. Moray (1969a) has recently opted for a modified filter theory model.

Treisman's Model

This model is primarily concerned with selective listening, although *mutatis mutandis* it can be made to apply to other modalities as well.

Suppose that several messages arrive at once over different input channels, and that the listener wishes to accept one and reject the others. The messages are first examined by sampling the various channels and analysing the simple physical characteristics such as pitch, loudness, time of arrival, location in space, etc. This is carried out on all messages, and the information from all messages is available to the listener at the level of consciousness. Simple physical characteristics are heard even from the rejected messages. This information is used by the filter to identify the channel which is to be selected. All other channels are then 'attenuated' (Treisman's word). This attenuation is not merely of signal amplitude, but of information or 'sensory evidence' (Treisman, personal communication), but she has not made clear just what the properties of the attenuation are, or how it works. Such a postulate is needed, however, since otherwise it is hard to see how *decrements* in signal intensity rather than increments could act as distractors, as is known to be the case in many experiments, both informal (the cessation of a clock's tick) and formal (Voronin and Sokolov, 1960, on dishabituation).

There would seem to be only two ways in which information in the Shannon sense could be 'attenuated': either by decreasing the signal intensity or by increasing the noise level. Both ways the S–N ratio would fall. But neither of these would cover the case of the decremental signal. Treisman's model needs to include an account of how the recoding is done which converts signal intensity into 'sensory evidence'. (For example, a network which took the modulus of the value of the signal might be satisfactory.) It seems to the writer that a much more likely model would be a running correlation on the basis of signal detection, as we shall see below. Treisman has not developed her ideas on these points, and at present the closest analogy we have for attenuation is the gain control in an audio-electronic circuit.

The effect of attenuating all messages except the desired one is to lower their signal-to-noise ratios, since noise is added at synapses later in the system, between the filter and the pattern analyser which handles complex discrimination.

The analyser therefore receives one full-strength message and one or more attenuated ones.

The pattern recognizer consists of 'dictionary units' which respond to patterns of input, providing the input is intense enough to pass the threshold of the appropriate recognizer. Although it is nowhere made explicit, it seems that the firing of a 'dictionary unit' corresponds to the conscious recognition of the stimulus by the listener. The thresholds of the dictionary units differ and are variable. Some have permanently lowered thresholds, such as those for a listener's own name. Hence, even if a message has been attenuated, providing it contains the listener's name, he will hear it. When a dictionary unit fires, the threshold of all other units which are probabilistically linked to that unit are transiently lowered, thus accounting for the context switching effects. Whichever unit fires gains access to the response mechanisms. In later versions of the model Treisman incorporates the concepts of 'analysers' from the theories of Sutherland (1964) and Mackintosh (1964) to describe how the various features of a signal may be independently processed. One problem for this system seems to be that it is possible for several dictionary units to fire simultaneously if their thresholds are appropriately matched to incoming signals along several channels, in which case the listener should hear several things at once. No predictions can be made as to what will happen if the listener is asked to handle two simultaneous inputs, accepting them both. No account is given as to the time constants of the switching mechanism and threshold changes. These latter two omissions make quantitative predictions difficult.

The Model of Deutsch and Deutsch

This model was proposed on the basis of the same experimental evidence as that used by Treisman, but maintains that her 'physical characteristic' analysers early in the system are redundant. All messages are fully analysed at the level of pattern recognition. The result of analysis is to produce an output from 'dictionary units' which is proportional, not to the signal strength of the input, but to its strength weighted by its importance to the organism. The weighting can be altered by long-term factors such as conditioning and reinforcement schedules, or by short-term factors such as the instructions given, or payoffs. A detailed account of the weighting mechanisms can be found in Deutsch (1960). The unit with the greatest weighted output gains access to the response system, including that part of the mechanism which subserves conscious perception. Conscious perception of a message is not synonymous with the firing of a pattern recognizer, but is a response to the output of a recognizer. The model has been called a response-selection model, but is not so regarded by Deutsch (1967, personal communication), who thinks of it as being the same kind of system as Treisman's dealing with selection among inputs. Recently a more elaborate version of this model has appeared in the work of Norman (1968, 1969) incorporating memory factors as well as attention.

## Discussion of the Models

Recently there has been a rather inconclusive struggle between the Treisman and Deutsch groups, with Broadbent's model being rather in the background as far as selective listening is concerned, although prominent in other fields of human performance theory. Experiments designed by Treisman to distinguish her model from Deutsch's have been hailed by both groups as supporting their respective positions. Some reasons for this have been discussed, with more detailed properties of the models by Moray (1969), and the basic difficulty seems to be that neither model has been described in sufficient detail and accuracy to make detailed prediction possible, in the sense of being able to predict the particular response on a particular occasion to a particular word within a message, rather than mere over-all trends averaged over whole messages, There are, however, three points which can be made.

Both Deutsch and Broadbent predict that simultaneous signals of equal strength and importance should lead to difficulties for the system, which operates by choosing one out of $n$ possible signals as that to which a response can be given at any moment. Treisman, as we saw above, makes no particular prediction about this. Secondly, neither Broadbent's model nor Deutsch's should have any difficulty in dealing with signals which alternate in time, so that a response is never required to both messages at once. The same is true of Treisman's model. Treisman's model explicitly states that 'crude physical characteristics' of the signals are analysed before the filter attenuates the undesired messages, and therefore performance on more than one message at a time should be possible providing that the message consist of 'crude physical characteristics' only.

Another source of difficulty is probably the use of shadowing as the method of presenting stimuli. Its popularity is to some extent due to an historical accident together with its extreme convenience. But with running speech as stimulus and response it is very difficult to look at the fine structure of stimulus–response relationships, and virtually impossible seriously to measure the effect of slight timing differences, which must surely be crucial for an understanding of attention. How long is a speech signal? Should we time its duration from the onset of the word, from the occurrence of a phoneme boundary, from the transition from one distinctive feature to another? The result is that typically over-all averaged scores are used which may hide as much as they reveal, and even when word-by-word analyses are attempted (e.g. Treisman and Geffen, 1967) their interpretation is difficult.

A further respect in which it seems likely that all the models are deficient is that they concentrate entirely upon competition between inputs. There is growing evidence that we may need to take into account competition among outputs, and between inputs and outputs, which none of the models is easily modifiable to cover. Moray and Taylor (1958), for example, noticed that listeners who were shadowing non-redundant prose (statistical approximations to English) omitted many of the words but claimed that they had heard them, as if the problem of receiving a difficult message prevented them from generating an output. There is also the problem of information transmission rate. If a listener shadows random digits, he will achieve a certain limiting rate of transmission. If he is now required to add a constant to each number before re-emitting it, or to translate it into French, or to emit not the current number but the last but two, his maximum rate of shadowing will fall markedly, although from the point of view of the input–output matrix the transmission rate is the same in each case, since there is a one-to-one translation. This problem has been discussed by Moray (1967, 1969) and related to stimulus–response compatibility (see also Posner, 1965).

On balance it seems likely that until some clarification and increased precision is achieved in the formulation of the models, and in particular until quantitative predictions can be extracted from them, it will be difficult to distinguish between them. However, there is reason to think that by then they will all have been found wanting, and to see why we shall examine some more experiments.

# 3 Some Attempts to Test the Models

Recently there have been several experiments which have tried to break away from shadowing as the means of analysing what happens in selection, and these look to be particularly good for testing the models. For one thing they allow that closer look at moment-by-moment details of performance, which we have already said will be needed to unravel the niceties of selection. So far the new experiments have failed to give unequivocal support to any of the models, but have at least introduced new ways of collecting data and new methods of analysis. It may well be that at present this is what is most needed in the development of research.

## Simultaneous Targets

Among the new methods is the use of logical AND stimulus configurations; that is, cases where stimuli are presented in two ongoing messages at the same time and responses required to *both*. Although some of the early 'question and answer' experiments used simultaneous presentation, the synchrony was of the entire message, rather than word by word within the sentences.

In retrospect it is rather strange that so little work has been done on AND stimuli, for the most common question which the man in the street might ask about attention is whether he can hear or do two things at once. Yet most research has been using an exclusive OR (XOR) paradigm, where responses are required to one or the other but not to both messages at the same instant. One obvious reason for this is that shadowing has been the most common experimental technique for collecting responses, and we cannot expect a listener to be able to speak two messages at once. But even when a tapping response to stimuli in one message has been combined with shadowing and tapping in the other (Treisman and Geffen 1967, 1968) the XOR mode of presentation has been used, in so far as a tapping response was never required simultaneously on both channels. ANDs can be used in either an inclusive OR (IOR) mode or alone (see Figure 4).

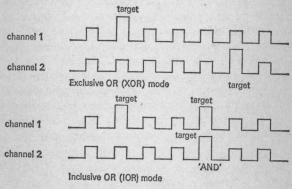

Figure 4 Modes of stimulus presentation

The only experiments which have looked at ANDs in continuous tasks have been those by Moray and O'Brien (1967) and Moray (1970a, 1970b). These studies have ceased to use shadowing as a way of locking the attention onto the desired message, and have relied instead upon rate of presentation to so load the listener that he will not shift his attention except deliberately. On the basis of these experiments it seems that shadowing is not required to obtain systematic results, although the price to pay may be the need for more sophisticated apparatus to control the experiment. Underwood (1971) has recently explored this point experimentally and come to the same conclusion.

*Shadowing with two responses*

Treisman and Geffen (1967) used the XOR mode. They required listeners to shadow one of a pair of dichotic prose messages. In addition certain words were nominated as critical words and the listeners asked to make a tapping response if they heard the crucial words either in the accepted or in the rejected messages. Suitable choice of words allowed them to compare the detectability, for example, of words which sounded alike with those whose meaning was the same. The results were interpreted by Treisman and Geffen as supporting their notion of partial attenuation somewhere along the afferent pathway. The number of tapping responses to target words in the rejected message was very much lower than to those in the accepted message. When a target in the accepted message was detected, there was little interference with shadowing, but on the occasion when rejected message targets were detected, there was substantial interference with shadowing.

The basis of their prediction was as follows. The tapping response, which they called the secondary response, was the same for both messages. Hence, if we interpret Deutsch's model to be a response model, the same response is to be given in both cases, and since the presentation is XOR mode, there will be no competition and performance on tapping should be equally good with respect to both messages. If, on the other hand, there is attenuation of one message, then the tapping and shadowing response to the primary message should be efficient, but the tapping response to the rejected message (the one not shadowed) should be poor. This is of course what they found.

Unfortunately, there are a number of alternative explanations. Deutsch and Deutsch (1967) have discussed some of them. Since one message is both shadowed and tapped, while the other is merely tapped, we could argue that this makes the listener regard the former as the more important, so that on the Deutsch model there is a greater importance weighting given to the shadowed message than to the non-shadowed message. Thereupon the Deutsch model predicts the observed outcome. Again, one might argue that the two responses involved are not shadowing on the one hand and tapping on the other, but rather shadowing-plus-tapping on the one hand and tapping only on the other. Again Deutsch's model then predicts the observed outcome. Since there was so little interference with shadowing when tapping responses were given to critical signals in the shadowed message, this last interpretation gains in plausibility. The experiment is, then, not a crucial one for distinguishing between the models.

Treisman and Geffen (1967), however, did provide a direct test of a prediction by the Deutsches which produced results supporting Treisman's rather than the Deutsch model. They also observed in passing that selection seemed to alter the signal detection theory statistic $d'$ rather than $beta$, a finding which had also been reported by Broadbent and Gregory (1964) in a slightly different experiment. The application of signal detection theory to continuous selective listening was taken further by Moray and O'Brien (1967). They omitted shadowing altogether, merely requiring listeners to tap a right hand key when they heard a target in the right ear, a left hand key when they heard a target in the left ear, and both keys when they heard targets in both ears. The messages consisted of long strings of random numbers, interspersed among which were random letters. The targets were the letters. They compared the condition where only one such message was presented with that in which two messages were presented dichotically but only one needed a response, and with the full IOR condition (left, right and both). They found that $d'$ again was the only statistic which showed systematic changes, and that in the select-one-reject-one situation it rose for the selected message and fell for the rejected message compared with the IOR value. However, if the responses were pooled and not regarded as two channels but only as a single detection task, there appeared to be 'conservation of $d'$' in that the value for the IOR condition was the same as for the selection-plus-rejection mode. All the $d'$ values were substantially lower than that for single channel conditions.

The main objection to this experiment is that it is difficult to justify some of the assumptions which have to be met for signal detection theory to be applied. Almost certainly they were not met. To name but one, there is something rather odd about regarding spoken digits as a noise distribution and letters as signals plus noise. Moreover, no one at the time of writing has produced ROC curves for different conditions of attention, and without such curves the application of signal detection theory measures runs into difficulties. Apart from the signal detection analysis, however, Moray and O'Brien reported another interesting statistic. In the IOR mode, where listeners were trying to handle both messages, there was a very high probability of detecting one member of an AND, but a very low probability of detecting both members. That is, listeners cannot, even when they try, handle ANDs.

This result would be predicted of course both by Deutsch's and Broadbent's model. But Treisman's makes no obvious prediction. The latter says that when a listener tries to accept one message and reject another he does so by attenuating the unwanted message. But no prediction follows for what happens when he tries to accept both. Are both attenuated? Or neither? Or only one? If the application of attenuation is optional, and only concerned with the exclusion of unwanted messages, then neither need be attenuated, and perfect performance on ANDs should result. This would conflict with Moray and O'Brien's result. If on the other hand both are attenuated, then performance on neither channel should be good, but it is all right on one. If from moment to moment first one and then the other is selected, then without more details of the mechanism we cannot make predictions. If, for example, there is a Broadbent switching filter before the attenuation mechanism, or in it, then Moray (1969) has shown that by suitably choosing the time constants the whole concept of partial attenuation can be made redundant, not by accepting Deutsch's model but by modifying Broadbent's original model. Loss of information due to a very rapid switch will, of course, produce behaviour which in most respects is indistinguishable from continuous partial attenuation, although certain critical experiments can be designed in principle.

Experiments with Pure Tones

The other experiments by Moray (1970a, 1970b) mark an even more radical departure from the shadowing work in that he no longer uses verbal signals at all, but pure tones. The experiments are part of a programme of research on two-channel psychophysics. Listeners are required, as in Moray and O'Brien's experiment, to respond to targets by pressing buttons. The signals are tone bursts, and the targets increments of loudness, pitch, changes in position, etc. Conditions investigated were single channel, select-one-and-reject the other, XOR and IOR (see Figure 5). Both with intensity and frequency increments there is a marked drop in the detection of targets in moving from the first two to the last two conditions. Deliberate time-sharing lowers performance. The drop in XOR performance would not be predicted by Deutsch and Deutsch's model (see p. 40) since the two responses are never required at the same instant. Once more ANDs are very poorly detected, although the probability of detecting one member of an AND is as good as performance in XOR. This contradicts the earlier views that crude physical characteristics are not treated in the same way as verbal stimuli, and suggests that those experiments be re-examined. On the other hand false alarms in all the two-channel conditions are far more often associated with the presentation of a target on the opposite channel than with the presentation of no target at all, which suggests that there is not a complete suppression of information from one channel when the other is being sampled.

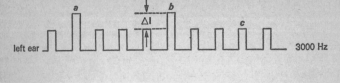

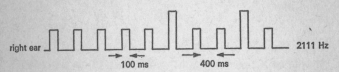

Figure 5 I O R mode of presentation in Moray's experiment. At *a* the listener should press the left-hand button, at *c* the right-hand button, and at *b* the 'both' button ; *b* is an A N D mode of presentation

Intuitively it might be expected that increasing the duration of the signals would make it possible to detect ANDs. There would be time to sample one channel, make a decision, and then change to the other channel and sample that one. But Moray found that while the detection of ANDs did indeed increase as the signal duration was changed from twenty-five milliseconds to 250 milliseconds, performance was extremely poor even at the latter duration. Indeed his curves relating hits to signal duration suggest that for some subjects signals would have to last for several seconds for the fact that they were both targets to be appreciated, a ridiculous suggestion. In his experiment there is no obvious calculation by which the probability of AND detections can be predicted. It conspicuously cannot be calculated by multiplying the joint probabilities of single target detections, the result being too low for most listeners.

It is worth speculating a little further about the relation between these results and the earlier opinion that simple physical signals, as distinct from ones with semantic content, were unaffected by selection. Lawson (1966), for example, played two prose messages to listeners and required them to shadow one. Mixed with the prose messages were tone bursts of 350 milliseconds duration and 750 Hz frequency. They occurred in both the rejected and the accepted message. She required listeners to shadow one message and give tapping responses to all tone bursts, and found that none were missed from the rejected message. This seems to contradict Moray's results quoted above. But a number of comments can be made about Lawson's experiment which may go far to resolving the discrepancy. In the first place her paper gives no details about the relative or absolute levels of intensity of the tone bursts with respect to the other material presented. Secondly, the tones were simply added to the ongoing speech message, so there must have been at least 6 dB or so increment in the power in the critical band centred on 750 Hz, which is well represented in speech. Next, there seems to have been no control over the rise-time of the tone bursts, so that there may have been prominent clicks produced either in the recording or by the non-linear transmission of the ear. The experiments by Moray used much more highly controlled stimuli, with computer controlled stimuli so that onset and offset were exactly simultaneous, and switching transients were suppressed. Moreover, Moray and Fee (1969) have repeated Lawson's experiment as closely as possible except that the tone bursts were shaped to avoid transients, and the speech was turned off at the moment that the tone bursts were turned on, so that the average acoustic power was kept approximately constant. They found that while about half of their subjects behaved like Lawson's, the others showed very markedly inferior performance in detecting pure tones in the non-shadowed ear. Some of the subjects remarked that the tones 'stood out' as though there was a sort of von Restorff effect operating. If, for example, attentional sampling was organized in such a way that a sample is taken whenever a marked change of any kind takes place in even an unattended channel, this would produce such an effect, and would go a long way to explaining many of the other results. (See Moray, 1969 for a discussion.) This would also account for the undoubted effect of decrements in signal intensity as targets, which is otherwise puzzling. Experiments on decrements are, incidentally, still very rare in the field of selective listening.

All in all, it is the opinion of the writer that at present the evidence is in favour of the view that at any moment the listener is either completely sampling one channel and completely ignoring the other, or vice versa. If there is partial attenuation, it is so severe as to be indistinguishable to all intents and purposes from complete blocking. On the other hand, the apparent indifference of the system to gross increases in signal duration when detecting AND signals is puzzling. At present there is no adequate theory of selective listening which will cover the experiments we have so far reviewed. More recent experiments on pure tones, similar to those described earlier, but much more extensive, seem to confirm the impression that the best model would be some kind of switching model similar to the one initially put forward by Broadbent (1958), and recently revised by him in his new book (1971). Probably an important variation is to assume that the switching is not regular and as fast as possible, but aperiodic and determined by the nature of the message which is being attended (Moray, 1972). Another important paper which has recently appeared in connexion with the topics discussed in this chapter is by Shaffer and Hardwick.

# 4 The 'Split-Span' Experiment

This experiment, or group of experiments, was introduced by Broadbent (1954). It is one of the most readily reproducible experiments in the whole of psychology, and is one of the most important experiments for establishing the Filter Theory which Broadbent supports. Although the original interpretation proposed by Broadbent is now in doubt, the experiment is important for other reasons, since the method lies on the borderline between the continuous tasks and the single presentation, question and answer kinds of experiment. Moreover, whereas the continuous tasks minimize the role of memory, the split-span task deliberately explores the role of memory in selection. It is as well to bear in mind therefore, when examining these experiments, that while there is no doubt that they throw light on the working of some selection mechanism, it remains to be established in each case whether the limits on performance are caused by selection during the original reception of the messages, or by selection operating on the short- or long-term memory store. In fact while there is little argument as to whether or not shadowing or key pressing detection tasks are concerned with reception, much of the theoretical discussion of the split-span task has centred on whether input or retrieval mechanisms are the cause of the limits.

The experiment as originally described by Broadbent consists in the presentation of three pairs of digits or other signals. The signals are presented in such a way that the listener hears the two members of each pair as nearly simultaneously as possible (AND mode), but no response is required until all three pairs of stimuli have been presented. At the end of the lists the subject is required to recall as many as he can, either in a specified order or by free recall.

Originally Broadbent used dichotic presentation, with one member of each pair going to one ear and the other to the other. The rate of presentation varied from two pairs per second to one pair per two seconds. He found that listeners tended to recall spontaneously ear by ear rather than alternating between the ears; that is, in the order L L L R R R rather than L R L R L R. Furthermore if listeners were asked to recall in the alternating mode, they showed very poor levels of performance if the presentation rate was faster than one pair every one-and-a-half-seconds. Measuring in terms of number of lists totally correct Broadbent found that in sequential recall there were very few errors, while alternating recall showed only about 20 percent of the lists totally correct. He concluded that this limit was due to the fact that with the convergence of information from the two ears on to the central limited capacity channel the rate at which the filter could alter the position of its switch was so slow that the alternating mode could not be handled. Two perceptions plus two switches take one-and-a-half seconds.

The major result, that at rates of presentation faster than about one pair every second listeners usually do very badly when recalling alternately from the two channels, is correct. It has also been found to hold for other dimensions of selection. For example, Moray and Barnett (1965) obtained the effect when a single loudspeaker was used to present the lists, but one member of each pair was spoken by a man and the other by a girl. The interpretation of the result is, however, much more controversial.

To begin with, we may notice that in other kinds of experiments the perception of spoken digits takes only a few tens of milliseconds. Thus Davis *et al.* (1961) asked listeners to repeat aloud single numbers which were spoken over headphones to them, in an echoic reaction-time task. Reaction times to the set of alternatives 0 – 9 were less than 250 milliseconds. Now if it takes only a quarter of a second to make a response to a heard digit, the time taken to receive and analyse it must be substantially shorter, let us say 180 milliseconds to be generous. Then two such perceptions will require only just over one-third of a second, and it appears that the time taken to switch attention must be well over half a second, which at least to the writer seems intuitively far too long to be plausible. (If it were correct there would be absolutely no possibility of ever handling AND stimuli in some of the experiments described in previous sections of this monograph.)

This objection is in line with a series of criticisms which Moray (1960) has levelled at Broadbent's interpretation. He found that with single-channel presentation, four digits per second could be recalled almost perfectly, and argued that this showed that the perception of single digits must take very much less than a quarter of a second. Furthermore, the distribution of errors within single sets of three pairs of digits does not seem to fit Broadbent's model; and the over-all error rate was far too low to fit the time constants of the hypothesized decaying-trace short-term memory store proposed by Broadbent.

Moray suggested that reception was in fact in parallel, and that there was no buffer store before the filter. Rather, the error pattern reflected difficulties arising during retrieval. However, Broadbent and Gregory (1961) presenting one member of each pair visually and the other auditorily found a large difference in performance depending on whether the mode of recall was specified before presentation or after, which Moray's interpretation would not have predicted.

## Ways of Scoring Errors

There is no doubt that one source of difficulty in comparing experiments lies in the different methods of scoring which are used by different workers. Thus Broadbent used the number of lists totally correct, while Moray scored the errors item by item. The trouble with the latter is that once an error has occurred in a list it is not clear what to do about the rest. For example, if the second item is missed out altogether, and totally correct recall is the criterion, should all the last items be considered wrong since they are in the wrong position? Or should only one omission be scored?

Moray and Barnett (1965), using male and female voices as the two channels, systematically investigated the differences obtained when different methods of scoring are used. They found that if only omissions are scored, then the sole significant source of variance was the rate of presentation of the stimuli. If only order errors were scored (lists, that is, where all the items were recalled but in the wrong order), then the only significant source of variance was strategy of recall (whether sequential or alternating). When number of lists totally correct was the criterion (that is the method used by Broadbent), then once again retrieval strategy was the only significant source of variance. They interpreted their results to mean that the different methods of scoring were tapping different parts of the mechanism. Specifically, they suggested that the recall strategy scores tapped output mechanisms while omissions tapped input mechanisms. If this is the case, then by using the appropriate scores we should be able to get a relatively 'pure' look at the different parts of the system. For example, if we could eliminate omission errors, then all the errors would reflect the performance of the recall mechanism. In an attempt to do this, they repeated the experiment using lists made up from the digits 1 – 6, so that all the possible stimuli were present on every trial, and the only problem for the listener was to report them in the correct order. To their surprise this produced the highest omission score of all, but also the pattern of errors changed, suggesting that the listeners were adopting a different strategy.

Moray and Beck therefore carried out the following experiment to determine to what extent the strategies used by the listeners could be deliberately manipulated.

*The effect of payoff on split-span performance*

The method was in general the same as that used by Moray and Barnett (1965). However, subjects were required on some runs to avoid omission errors and on others to avoid order errors. The aim was to show firstly that one kind of error could be eliminated without affecting the other, and secondly that this could be related to mechanisms of reception or retrieval, depending on the kind of error.

The two sets of instructions to the listeners were as follows:

(1) You will win 6d. for each set of six completely correct digits, but lose 1d. for every number left out. If you put in a wrong number or get the numbers in the wrong order but all present you will neither gain or lose anything. So if in doubt, guess. If, at the end of the experiment you have lost more than you have won, you will be paid nothing.

(2) In this experiment you will win 6d. for each set of completely correct digits but lose 6d. for each set of digits which is in the wrong order. If you are in doubt leave a blank, in which case you will neither win nor lose anything. If at the end of the experiment you lose more than you win you will be paid nothing.

As in the earlier experiment both a large ensemble, in which six digits were selected from 0 to 9 for each list, and a small ensemble, in which all the members of 1 to 6 were present on each trial, were used. Two rates of presentation, one pair per second and two pairs per second were used. And two strategies of recall, sequential and alternating, were required of the subjects, the latter being told before each series of lists which type of recall to use. The results are summarized in Tables 1, 2, and 3.

The experiment was at least partly successful. It is certainly possible to alter the relative proportions of the different kinds of errors by altering the payoff to the listener. The results of the analysis of variance are not so clear-cut as in

Table 1
Mean Error Scores per Ten Lists in Different Conditions of Payoff in a Split-Span Experiment for Two Stimulus Ensembles

| | At least one error per list | | Order errors | | Omissions | | Commissions | |
|---|---|---|---|---|---|---|---|---|
| Stimulus ensemble: | 6 from 10 | 6 from 6 | 6 from 10 | 6 from 6 | 6 from 10 | 6 from 6 | 6 from 10 | 6 from 6 |
| Avoid omissions | 7·83 | 6·66 | 2·61 | 5·11 | 8·27 | 2·16 | 5·22 | 1·22 |
| Unpaid | 6·80 | 5·50 | 2·27 | 2·75 | 6·17 | 6·05 | 2·27 | 0·90 |
| Avoid order errors | 8·44 | 6·94 | 1·33 | 1·88 | 32·22 | 26·55 | 2·11 | 0·33 |

Table 2
Analysis of Variance for the Large Ensemble (six digits chosen from ten)

| Lists with at least one error | | Order errors | |
|---|---|---|---|
| Recall | $p < 0.01$ | Between subjects | $p < 0.01$ |
| Presentation rate | $p < 0.05$ | Payoff strategy | $p < 0.01$ |
| | | Recall | $p < 0.01$ |
| | | Payoff x recall | $p < 0.05$ |
| | | Presentation rate | $p < 0.05$ |
| Omissions | | Commissions | |
| Between subjects | $p < 0.05$ | Payoff strategy | $p < 0.05$ |
| Payoff strategy | $p < 0.01$ | | |
| Presentation rate | $p < 0.01$ | | |

All sources of variance reaching $p < 0.05$ or better are shown.

Table 3
Analysis of Variance for the Small Ensemble (six digits chosen from six)

| Lists with at least one error | | Order Errors | |
|---|---|---|---|
| Between subjects | $p < 0.05$ | Payoff strategy | $p < 0.01$ |
| Recall | $p < 0.01$ | Recall | $p < 0.05$ |
| Omissions | | Commissions | |
| Between subjects | $p < 0.05$ | Payoff strategy | $p < 0.05$ |
| Payoff strategy | $p < 0.01$ | | |
| Presentation rate | $p < 0.01$ | | |
| Payoff x presentation rate | $p < 0.05$ | | |
| Recall x presentation rate | $p < 0.05$ | | |
| Payoff x recall x presentation rate | $p < 0.05$ | | |

All sources of variance reaching $p < 0.05$ or better are shown.

the earlier experiment, which was free from interaction effects. Another point emerges when we compare the two experiments, which is very interesting. The condition called
'Unpaid' in Table 1 is taken from the earlier experiment,
and represented what happens when listeners are left to
their own devices as to what strategy and payoff they will
adopt. It is clear that when left to themselves they behave so
as to minimize omissions. This makes sense, for unless omissions are minimized high scores cannot be obtained. If one
makes no omissions, there is at least a chance that one will
produce a perfect response, even if guessing is used. But any
omissions mean that there is no possibility of being completely correct. Most errors in 'unbiased' listeners will therefore be order errors, and will be affected by recall strategy
(which Moray and Barnett argue are retrieval errors). If
Broadbent had scored omissions instead of lists totally correct, he would have tapped the other source of errors, and
might never have concluded that switching time was important. It seems likely that the effect of rate of presentation on recall is indirect, perhaps due to the fact that at fast
rates there is less time for rehearsal and consolidation between items. There is also informal evidence in substantial
quantities that listeners tend to recall at a fast rate when
presentation is fast and at a slow rate when presentation
is slow, so that in all experiments paced recall should be
used.

As time has passed the interpretation of the split-span task
has become increasingly complicated. Moray and Jordan
(1966) pointed out that strictly speaking neither sequential
nor alternating recall is recall 'in the correct order of arrival' as Broadbent originally stated. To recall in the correct
order of arrival requires the listener to write or speak two
messages at once. This is a skill at which few are proficient.
Without it, the split-span task forces the listener to perform
at least one extra transform on the signals he receives,
namely parallel-to-serial conversion. It may be that the
limits on performance are set by the proficiency of this re-

coding rather than by input sampling rates or retrieval mechanisms.

*Effects of practice and other variables*

Moray and Jordan (1966) trained listeners to use a stenographic keyboard, which allows more than one key to be pressed at once. Listeners could thus type what they heard in their left ear with the left hand and what they heard with their right ear with their right hand. Furthermore, the subjects were given many more trials than in any of the previous experiments. Using Broadbent's criterion of trials completely correct, they found that in over one hundred trials their subjects reached performance levels where they obtained over 80 per cent correct when making simultaneous manual responses, with presentation rates of two pairs per second. In addition they found that with this amount of practice their subjects included several who achieved better than 80 per cent correct using a verbal alternating response, a striking reversal of the percentages usually found by workers using less practised subjects.

This question of practice is extremely important. Perhaps because listeners reach fairly stable rates of responding within relatively few trials in selective listening experiments, at least as measured by the rather crude methods so far employed, little or no work has been done on the effects of sustained practice. Few people have shadowed more than a few hundred words, or recalled more than a few dozen lists in split-span experiments. There is a real need for these experiments to be repeated with much more highly practised subjects, especially if the information is to be used to assess communication systems in real-life situations. As already mentioned, most experimenters know that over a year or two of working in the field their own levels of performance increase greatly. We know far too little about the effects of practice.

Further complexities in the split-span experiment come from the work of Gray and Wedderburn (1960). They used material which came from different verbal classes, instead of having all the signals composed of digits. Thus a typical sextet might be:

| Left ear: | seven | aunt | four |
| Right ear: | dear | nine | Jane |

They found that recall of the lists class by class was as efficient as sequential, ear-by-ear recall. Bryden (1964) reported a similar effect when working with stimuli which were related by associative links of different strengths. Items with high associative-link strength tended to be grouped together regardless of the order in which they had been presented. Broadbent and Gregory (1964) found that Gray and Wedderburn's result held even when neither of the lists had marked semantic content, using lists of the form:

| Left ear: | q | five | h |
| Right ear: | four | s | seven |

so that the grouping effect is not due to the continuity of meaning, but seems to be related to the signals being members of different classes whose members in some sense form a psychologically unified group. They noted, however, that in their and in Gray and Wedderburn's experiment the lack of difference between class and sequential grouping was due to the abnormally low recall in the sequential mode, rather than a strikingly high efficiency in the classification mode of recall.

Savin (1967) used lists which contained only four items. A single speaker recorded each of them singly, and at different times, so that there was no 'continuity' from the first to the second member of a pair. All four members of a quartet were presented over a single loudspeaker in two pairs, with all the cues for separating or organizing them reduced to an absolute minimum. Listeners still tended to report them as two sequential pairs, rather than pair by pair with alternation between members of the same pair. He concluded that the tendency to sequential organization was an inherent property of the auditory system, organized as it seems to be for receiving input which is usually sequential in nature and lasts for some time (for example, spoken sentences). On the other hand, Day (1967) found that if the material presented to opposite ears was in some sense complementary there was a tendency to fusion. She presented pairs of 'words' to opposite ears:

| | | | |
|---|---|---|---|
| Left ear: | Poduct | Right ear. | Roduct |
| Left ear: | Coset | Right ear: | Loset |

These were reported respectively as *product* and *closet*. Moreover when asked to recall the input to one ear only, without the material to the other ear being present, recall was accurate, i.e. *roduct* or *loset* rather than the synthesized word, suggesting that the effect was not due to guessing, but to genuine fusion. This belief is strengthened by the fact that listeners reported that the sound image was centralized. A similar experiment using non-verbal stimuli, which casts light on the limits of fusion, can be found in Broadbent (1955).

Bryden (1962) has discussed in detail some of the response patterns which are obtained in split-span experiments. If listeners are left to themselves a wide variety of responses are seen which, apart from sequential and alternating, may include 'Knight's move' patterns and many others (L L R R R L, L R R L L R, etc.). He tends to the view favoured by the present writer that the most important mechanisms involved are retrieval ones rather than input selection ones. One would expect that if the most important factor is input selection and switching then rate of presentation would be the most critical factor. But the evidence is confusing. Moray (1960) found that overall errors, measured item by item, decreased with decreasing presentation rate for sequential recall. Bryden found the opposite (1962, 1964). Broadbent found that the result depended upon the population of subjects. Naval volunteers showed Bryden's effect, while members of Broadbent's research institute showed Moray's result (Broadbent and Gregory, 1964).

## Explanation of Split-Span Performance

It seems no longer possible to interpret the split-span experiment as Broadbent originally did, as a measure of switching-time between channels identified with afferent sensory systems or dimensions of the stimulus. Either the switch selects much more complex channels or dimensions or transforms of information (such as grammatical classes and languages), or there is a hierarchy of selective mechanisms. There is good evidence for high-level selection of languages in the work of Kolers (1968). Broadbent and Gregory found similar effects to those described when two classes of material were presented through one ear. In *Perception and Communication* Broadbent had proposed that verbal classes could be selected, but as then described it was difficult to see how they could be selected since as Moray (1960) pointed out verbal classes do not in general have physical features common to all their members which distinguishes them from other classes. The dichotic experiments raise this possibility afresh, however, and in so doing raise equally the location of the level in the nervous system at which selection takes place, and whether indeed it is at input rather than in retrieval (Yntema and Trask, 1963). In the present writer's opinion, the evidence at present available suggests that limits on split-span performance are more closely related to the properties of short-term memory than to attention mechanisms. But the final account of these phenomena is far from being conclusively established.

Other Split-Span Studies

The task has been used for a number of other purposes than the theoretical analysis of selective mechanisms. Thus Inglis (1960, 1961) and Kimura (1961a and b) have used it as a means of assessing brain damage. It has been remarked by Teuber (1962) among others that patients who seem to have little or no functional loss when tested with single channel tasks often show very marked decrements in their ability to handle more than one source of information at a time. It is rather as if damage to the brain reduces the size of a general purpose central processor (Moray, 1967; Posner, 1965). Inglis has studied both the effects of age and mental illness on split-span performance. Kimura's work has provided a series of studies on cerebral dominance in relation to selective listening, and there now is sufficient evidence to warrant the generalization that there are small but consistent differences between right and left sides of the brain when dichotic inputs are presented to the two ears. Performance seems to be better when the left ear is used for non-verbal stimuli, and when the right is used for verbal stimuli (Broadbent and Gregory, 1964; Kimura, 1961b, 1964; Treisman and Geffen, 1968). Perhaps the most striking claim of this kind to date is that of Shankweiler and Studdart-Kennedy (1967) that CV diagrams are better recognized with right ear presentation and intoned vowels by left ear presentation.

At least one experiment has extended split-span method to more than two channels. Moray *et al.* (1965) presented up to four stimuli over each of up to four channels. In the most difficult condition the listeners heard sixteen letters of the alphabet within two seconds, four over each channel. There was less evidence of channel by channel sequential recall when more than two channels were used. Rather, listeners seemed to give all the signals from one channel and then to recall in a rather disorganized way from the remaining material at their disposal. The number of items did not show a trading relation with the number of channels. Two items presented over each of four channels caused subjects to produce a worse performance than four items presented over each of two channels. Masking played only a minor role, since if asked in advance to listen only to one channel listeners were able to recall almost perfectly. When post-presentation cueing indicated which single channel was to be recalled, an auditory Sperling effect was observed, but not so dramatic a one as Sperling found in vision. The latter (Sperling, 1960) presented to observers three rows of letters and numbers one above the other in a tachistoscope. When each row contained four letters, recall of the whole array was rather poor, well below the traditional 'immediate memory span'. However, if immediately after the visual presentation a high, medium or low tone sounded to inform the observer which row he was to recall, then there was a dramatic improvement in the percentage of letters recalled, such that the evidence suggested that more than the usual span was present for very short intervals. Moray and O'Brien found that such cueing in the auditory modality restored the span to its usual single channel value, but requiring recall in the correct order of presentation as well as recall of the items had a catastrophic effect upon performance.

Moray and Reid (1967) tried to bridge the gap between dichotic split-span tasks and continuous tasks, since an earlier experiment by Moray and Jordan (1966) has suggested that if there was high compatibility between the input and the output split-span performance was greatly improved. Moray and Reid presented strings of dichotic pairs of letters and numbers using from two to five pairs per list, and compared the result with single channel strings of the same total number of items. The two-channel task was always less efficient than the single channel task, even when each hand had its own keyboard with which to respond. There was no obvious discontinuity in performance when the number of items exceeded the memory span.

It will be noticed that from the original neat and convincing experiment of Broadbent the split-span task has spread across ever wider conceptual fields, and the picture now is very much less clear than it was ten years ago. We probably need a new insight, at present unavailable, to combine the many and diverse experiments. The facts are fairly clear but their interpretation is extremely difficult.

Recently several important papers by Treisman have appeared which add further to our data in this area (1970; Treisman and Riley, 1969; Treisman, 1971).

# 5 The Time Taken to Switch Attention

We have at present no estimate of how long it takes to switch attention. This is partly due to the difficulties involved in formulating the question, and partly to the difficulties of timing internal events. Consider the extreme case of listening to one of a pair of dichotic messages presented to one ear, and then switching to listen to the other presented through the opposite ear. Now imagine a case when the sound sources are separated only by 10° in auditory space, and ask the listener to switch from one to the other. Would we expect it to take longer than the first case, or shorter, or the same? Since the 'distance' involved is only conceptual, and probably not a real distance between neurons, why should we expect there to be any difference? What we mean by switching must be some rearrangement of the pattern of excitation and inhibition in the nervous system, reflected in a changed probability of responses to the different sources of messages. There is, in a strict sense, no such thing as 'attention' which is 'switched'. The popular analogy of a searchlight sweeping the environment is totally misleading.

It is empirically apparent that some kinds of switching involve mechanisms, whatever they are, with very different time constants from others. For example, Kolers (1968) has shown that the time taken to switch from handling messages in one language to handling them in another seems to be of the order of seconds. The time taken to alter the criterion according to which lists of words are being searched is rather shorter (Neisser, 1967). What then would we expect to be the order of magnitude of the time taken to switch from listening with one ear to listening with the other, or from listening to a male voice to listening to a female voice? And is the same switch involved?

## Attempts to Measure Switching Time

There are four quite different attempts which have been made to determine the switching constants. In looking at them it is important to bear in mind the ambiguity in the phrase 'rate of switching attention'. It may mean either, 'How many times per second can I switch attention?', or it may mean, 'Having ceased to select one message, how long is it before the listener begins to handle the other?' The first problem is to measure the rate of cycling of the selection mechanism, the second to do with whether there is a 'dead time' in the switch, and if so what its duration is. It is not immediately obvious that there need be any dead time in a non-mechanical system. It could be that switching is reflected by a smoothly changing shift in the probability of transmitting the two messages, one probability continuously rising as the other falls, rather than by a step function of time such as is usually associated with, say, an electromechanical relay.

The importance of the distinction is that while a long dead-time necessarily produces a low switching rate in cycles per second, a short one will not necessarily allow a high rate, since there may be a minimum dwell time (MDT) for which the system must stay in a state once it has entered it. (This is similar to Broadbent's 'perception time' concept in the split-span task). The only quantity which we can readily measure behaviourally is the combination of the two, MDT and switching time. Even this has not been measured for certain. Most workers who have discussed attentional models seem to have assumed that switching is a step function, but this is clearly not necessarily so.

The first attempt to measure switching time was a very direct one by Cherry and Taylor (1954). They switched a message rapidly to and fro between the ears without synchronizing the switch with the onset of the words comprising the message, and found a marked drop in intelligibility at about three to four cycles per second. Unfortunately their argument that this was because the switch could not follow at this rate was vitiated by the discovery that merely turning the message on and off in one ear at the same rate produced a comparable loss in intelligibility, and that the critical rate seemed to be related to syllabic rate, suggesting that the effect was to do with the timing of critical features in the speech wave rather than switching (Huggins, 1964). Schubert and Parker (1955) found that the loss of intelligibility was less if noise was switched in antiphase with the speech, a finding whose meaning is not clear.

The second attempt to measure switching time was, as we have seen, the split-span experiment of Broadbent (1954, 1958). We have seen that the interpretation of these experiments is very difficult, and in particular to estimate the switching time or rate from them assumes that we can separate perception time and switching time. Since it seems unlikely that there is such a thing as *a* single perception time, this approach is of doubtful value, especially with the new appreciation of the role of 'ikonic' and 'echoic' storage (Neisser, 1967).

*Kristofferson's estimate.* A third attempt to measure switching time was made by Kristofferson, using reaction times. At first sight it looks a very attractive method, but in fact it will only work if certain assumptions built into the design are met, and the experiment itself does not test the assumptions, only deductions from them. Kristofferson presented two signals which began together, one a light and one a tone. After a short delay one of them ended. The task of the observer was to press a key if one of the pair ended, and to refrain from pressing it if the other ended. Reaction times were compared under conditions where the observer knew in advance which was to end and where he was uncertain, allowance being made for the difference in basic reaction times to visual and auditory signals. Kristofferson argued that in the uncertain condition the observer would, at any moment, be either sampling the visual or the auditory modality. Hence there was a 0·5 probability of being on the correct channel at the moment that the signal ended. If the observer was on the wrong channel, then he would begin his response when next he sampled that channel. He supposed that switching time was negligible, but that there was an MDT which he was trying to measure. The distribution of increased reaction times in the uncertain condition reflected the distribution of delays before the observer could sample the correct channel, and could be used to estimate the MDT.

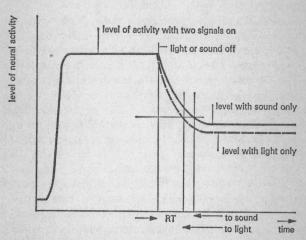

Figure 6 Kristofferson's experiment. In the uncertain case, the subject merely detects a departure from the 'two signals on 'level, as in the certain case. The experiment becomes a choice RT experiment rather than an experiment on attention switching

In fact in the two alternative situations there was no difference between the certain and the uncertain condition. When the number of alternatives was increased to four, of which two called for a response, he did find a difference which led him to conclude that the minimum dwell time, or sampling time, was of the order of sixty-five milliseconds, a full cycle therefore requiring about 130 milliseconds.

The main difficulty in accepting this estimate lies in the fact that it is possible to interpret it merely as a rather unusual choice reaction-time experiment, and unless we wish to say that all choice reaction-time experiments are properly regarded as attention-switching experiments, (a line which the present writer would not want to take), there is no compulsion about accepting Kristofferson's interpretation. Since this experiment is perhaps the best so far that has attempted to measure the time constants of attention, it is worth pursuing this point in some detail. To do so shows just how complex are the conceptual issues involved in attention research.

Consider what happens. Two signals begin simultaneously, their joint onset acting as a warning signal. After an interval of the order of a second one signal ceases, and if it is the specified one the observer is to make a response. If the MDT is fixed (or at least can be described by the parameters of some distribution), and if the time for which an observer must sample a channel must be multiples of the unit MDT, and if above all he can only sample one of the channels at a time, then Kristofferson's analysis may well be correct, although the value he suggests for the MDT makes it hard to see why Moray and O'Brien's (1967) subjects could not respond to ANDs. There is also the assumption that the switching time is negligible, but if this is incorrect it will merely add a constant to the obtained value of the MDT. The most serious assumption is that the listener must sample only one channel at a time. As we saw earlier, Moray's data (see pp. 43–50) support this assumption, although the values found by Kristofferson are not supported; but it is a matter of empirical evidence whether it is true or not, and the point being made here is that in Kristofferson's account it is actually an assumption, not an empirically established fact.

Suppose that in addition to transmitting modality-specific information through the respective primary afferent pathways an incoming signal also feeds information to some integrating device which monitors from moment to moment the total, over-all level of activity in all incoming sensory pathways. (It is known, for example, that all primary afferent pathways send collaterals to the reticular system, which could thus act as an information pool.) Kristofferson's results could then arise as follows.

Before either signal begins the information pool is relatively quiet, and altered only by moment-to-moment random fluctuations. When the signals begin the activity jumps to a high level, and when one of them ends it drops to an intermediate level, which will in general depend on which one ends. All the observer need do is to monitor the level of activity in the information pool. There is nothing which compels one to make the basic assumption which Kristofferson makes about the inability of the observer to sample more than one source of information at a time at some level in the nervous system.

Similarly there is an alternative explanation for his multiple-signal case. If four signals begin, and one of them ceases, the experiment is like an end-of-signal choice reaction-time task, where the four signals are the triads left by removing one signal from the tetrad which initially is turned on. The times found by Kristofferson agree rather well with this interpretation. For further discussion of these points see Kristofferson (1967a and b) and Moray (1969).

A final point which should be mentioned is that there are a number of experiments where the occurrence of simultaneous signals actually *improves* performance in the task of detecting one of them. It is a common finding in psychophysics that a simultaneous or even post-stimulus cue aids the detection of threshold signals. Like Kristofferson's experiments these are 'one shot' experiments, in which the listener prepares to receive a signal, receives it, and then responds; after which there is a pause and the cycle repeats. It may well be that different phenomena appear when such experiments are compared with the continuous, heavy-load tasks such as shadowing and steady-state detection experiments, where runs, rather than discrete trials are used.

The last attempt to measure switching time has already been mentioned. It is that of Moray's AND presentations with pure tones. When signals begin and end simultaneously, ANDs are very difficult to detect. Moray hoped that by varying the signal duration he could find a duration at which ANDs were never detected, and a longer duration where they were always detected, and that the former would measure the sampling time, and the difference the switching time. However, over a range of signal durations from twenty-five to 250 milliseconds there was only a smooth and rather slight increase, with neither perfect performance nor zero performance within the range of signals studied. This result is extremely puzzling. If there is a minimum dwell time, or a limited changeover time, we would surely expect that increasing the signal duration from twenty-five to 250 milliseconds would allow time for Moray and O'Brien's subjects to report the simultaneous occurrence of two letters in their 1967 experiment (see p. 45 above). It seems extremely unlikely that sampling must continue for as long as a quarter of a second or more on one particular channel. The relative ineffectiveness of long signals in allowing the detection of ANDs probably should be interpreted to mean that is in the early parts of the signals that the crucial information lies. For example, perhaps it is not the size of the signal increment that matters so much as its rate of onset. If two signals begin together with the same rate of onset, then functionally they would present only one increment, thus accounting for the difficulty in detecting ANDs. Or if the listener does switch, then if his switch is relatively slow, and does not produce a step-function in the onset of the second stimulus to be sampled, functionally it will behave as if it has a rather gentle onset, and is a weak signal. If it is the onset of signals which is crucial, many features of selective listening experiments might be explicable.

Consider the experiments of Lawson (1966) which we discussed earlier (p. 49), and which seems to show that tone bursts without smooth onsets and matched for equivalent loudness to the message in which they are embedded are unusually detectable. Now the waveforms of spoken words have in general rather slow onsets, while pressing a switch to complete a circuit and record a pure tone burst will produce a sharp rise in the leading edge of the burst, almost certainly with marked transients present. Suppose that a running average over a period of milliseconds is kept, and sudden departures from this call for a sample to be taken. Then the much sharper rise of the leading edge of the tone signals will cause them to be unduly detectable, although the mechanism involved handles them exactly as it handles the speech. If this is so, truly synchronized speech signals should be much harder to handle in a split-span experiment than the approximately synchronized signals prepared by the efforts of human experimenters. Triesman played some computer synchronized speech to the present writer and is currently working with this material, and judging by the present writer's experience it is much harder to listen to than traditional split-span material. When shadowing, such a mechanism will return rapidly to the correct message every time it has been forcibly called to the wrong one, so that little information will be acquired about the wrong message. But it might well be enough to distinguish 'crude physical characteristics' while being insufficient to convey the content of the message.

We shall develop some of these last mentioned ideas in the final chapter. For the present we must regretfully conclude that we still know little about switching time. Looking over the list of experiments, all designed to measure the same thing, one is struck by their diversity as much as by the difficulty of accepting any of them as valid estimates of what they set out to measure. Perhaps we have not yet thought sufficiently about what would constitute an answer. The problem remains obscure, and unsolved.

# 6 The Physiology of Selective Listening

Despite the fact that the search for the neural basis of selective listening has been in full swing now for a number of years, and the considerable amount of work that has been done, it must be admitted that the results are on the whole disappointing.

Over the entire field there is a shadow which is hard to dispel, and that is a doubt that we really know what it is that we should look for. What are the physiological indices which we should seek when a listener selects one message and rejects another? Confronted by so elaborate a mechanism as the human brain, there is a great temptation to oversimplify, fall back on analogy, and take for granted as obvious and necessary assumptions what are in fact highly debatable intuitions.

Perhaps the truth is that until we know much more about the general principles of coding which are used by the nervous system we will not be able to understand what we see when we record from it; and yet those very changes which we see are the only way to discover the coding rules. It is a classical problem of trying to lift oneself up by one's own bootstraps. Maybe we are lucky to be working at a time when the development of recursive procedures in many fields of computation has made that activity slightly more respectable than it once was.

## The Interpretation of Evoked Potentials

The most intuitively obvious expectation with regard to selective listening is certainly that if there are two messages presented to the nervous system, and if the listener wishes to accept one and reject the other, then the neurons through which the rejected message passes will be inhibited. Then we will expect to see a reduction in the size of the evoked potential which we can record from those pathways carrying the rejected message. But even if this were true, where should we look for such a reduction? Beyond the cochlear nucleus the input from each ear is represented on both sides of the brain. There is extensive but not complete crossing over from one side of the brain to the other of nerve pathways from each ear, and each auditory cortex receives input from both sides.

Some experiments have shown the suppression of one input by another. Thus Rosenweig and his co-workers (see, for example, Rosenweig and Wyers, 1955) showed that the earlier of two clicks, if delivered monaurally in the cat, would suppress the size of the evoked response to a later click delivered to the contralateral ear. Such interaction was found at almost every synapse of the afferent pathway. But what would we expect to see when the stimuli are not short clicks, but continuous prose messages, complex sound waves which carry both physical and semantic information to human listeners? If we assume that each input inhibits the other there would be a tremendously complex shifting pattern of transient changes reflecting inhibition and facilitation, in which it would be quite impossible to sort out the components of one message from those of the other with the technical resources at our disposal today. If selection were to occur far out in the periphery, before cross-over had occurred, then the chances of finding the specific effects of attention might be better, although we would still have to distinguish the effects of contralateral inhibition caused by the input to the opposite ear from central afferent control descending from the higher levels of the nervous system, and from masking of later parts of the ipsilateral message by its own earlier signals.

A much more serious problem arises from our lack of knowledge of the coding rules and principles of transmission in the nervous system. Most workers on attention seem to have made the assumption that a decrease in the size of the evoked potential in the afferent pathway or at a nucleus (including the cortex) would imply a weakening of the signal strength of the incoming message, and imply that the reception and analysing mechanisms were facing a decrease in the signal-to-noise ratio. Hence they have been concerned to show that when an animal is distracted the size of the evoked response decreases. Now if a gross macroelectrode is used, so that signals are picked up from a number of nerve fibres in a single nerve, then as the strength of stimulation increases, so that firing in each fibre is more frequent, the size of the evoked potential will also increase. But this is a dangerous premise on which to base research and our expectations about the effects of attention. Compare, for example, the magnitude of the voltages which can be recorded in the EEG of sleep, and the waking EEG. The huge synchronized discharges of deep, delta-wave sleep are among the highest non-pathological voltages which can be recorded, and yet the organism is almost totally unresponsive. If we were to assume that size of evoked potential was an index of activity, we would have to conclude that the human observer is intellectually most lively when he is fastest asleep.

The analysis of the central nervous system in terms of the behaviour of single cells has made remarkable progress in recent years. But for our purposes we require much more to know how long complex messages are represented in entire networks of many millions of cells. We know that the effect of increased intensity of stimulation on a single neuron is to increase the rate of firing. But we do not know how this information may be transformed and recoded in the depths of the brain. If, for example, intensity was ultimately read by a network of rate-counting cells in which the cell which gave an output was the one which registered the intensity, but *which* cell that was depended upon the intensity of the input, then there would be no change in the apparent evoked response from the network with changes of applied intensity.

Only if we could tell *which* cell was firing could we determine the effective intensity of the stimulus from there on into the further reaches of the nervous system. We have of course no reason to think that such a network exists: but until we do know how intensity is represented we cannot hope to measure the relative effective intensities of accepted and rejected messages. In the meantime we would be rash to equate a decrease in the evoked potential with a weaker signal: very often desynchronization is a sign of activity rather than loss of information.

Explicitly, it has been known for many years that there is only a weak correlation between physiological and behavioural indices of attentional states. It has been reported in several studies that while there is usually very rapid habituation to a repeated stimulus when habituation is measured behaviourally, it may take hours or even days longer for physiological habituation to appear, if cortical response is taken as the index. Indeed in one study (Sharpless and Jasper, 1956) it was found that when cats listened to repeated clicks the cortical response even after days did not disappear, and sometimes actually *increased* as the behavioural response declined. High voltage cortical evoked responses are not then to be taken as indicating behaviourally important events in the life of the animal. Probably perceptually important events require the simultaneous interaction of many different parts of the brain, in particular the cortex and the reticular activating system (Samuels, 1959).

The Work of Hernández-Peón

Such considerations are especially relevant in connexion with some of the most famous physiological experiments on attention, those of Hernández-Peón and his group (see Hernández-Peón, 1966, for a review). Typical of their studies was one where electrodes were chronically implanted in the cochlear nucleus of a cat, and the animal then placed in a box where it listened to clicks. The size of the cochlear nucleus evoked response was recorded. A mouse in a glass bowl was introduced into the box, or fish odour was blown into it, and the evoked response was observed to diminish, returning to normal when the distracting stimulus was withdrawn.

There are a number of things wrong with this experiment, and while we shall only examine the details of the experiments on hearing, similar objections can be made to the work of this group in other sensory modalities. The auditory experiments have been strongly criticized by Worden (1967) and Horn (1965). To begin with the magnitude of the changes observed was extremely small, and of the same order of size as other workers have found among spontaneous fluctuations. Moreover, only two or three recordings were reproduced in the papers, and there was no averaging of responses to increase the signal-to-noise ratio and reliability of the records. Nor were the records scored blind as an alternative. Next, the experiment has proved remarkably resistant to efforts to repeat it. Worden and his group tried for several years, but found themselves unable to do so, and furthermore discovered on closer inspection some rather remarkable aberrations from what one might expect. For example, they recorded from both the cochlear nuclei of the same animal, and found that sometimes when it was 'distracted' the evoked response in one cochlear nucleus increased when that in the other decreased. Careful analysis has suggested that the changes are more likely to be related to physical acoustics of the animals' environment than to attention. If the middle ear muscles are cut, and if the animals wear headphones, then the changes reported by Hernández-Peón do not appear. It seems that non-homogeneities in the sound field caused by, for example, standing waves in the box, are responsible. When the cat orientates to the distracting object, its ears take up new positions in the acoustic field, and because of the non-homogeneities the ears receive different stimulation, and hence the evoked response alters. It is certain that the box which Hernández-Peón's animal was in when the photographs in his paper were taken is far from unechoic. (A similar effect may be observed when a human listener sits near a television set. The faint high-pitched whistle which the set emits will be observed to change markedly in loudness if the head is turned back and forth, thus changing one's relation to the standing wave pattern of sound in the room, altering the head shadow, etc.)

The above and other criticisms have been elaborated in the papers mentioned. Taken as a whole we must conclude with regret that none of Hernández-Peón's experiments was reliably controlled. One of the problems is that the observed changes were so plausible, so much just what one would have suspected would happen. Worden has expressed this well in describing the events which led to his rejection of the Hernández-Peón work:

... throughout our experimental work a prominent relationship between amplitude of auditory potentials ... and position of ears in space was persistently attributed to behavioural variables ... as the animal oriented to the overhead speaker ... the accompanying change in amplitude would be interpreted to reflect the shift of attention to the auditory signal ... as the animal moved progressively through the positions of standing alert, sitting with drooping head, and finally lying down and curling up, the concomitant amplitude changes were assumed to relate variously to levels of arousal and direction of attention.... Recognition of the significance of ear position in terms of acoustic variations within the sound field was finally forced upon us by observations which defied even imaginative interpretation (Worden, 1967, p. 75).

While most of the experiments specifically designed to look for the peripheral control of afferent inflow must therefore be dismissed, there are hints as to where the mechanisms may lie, and the hints suggest on the whole that, however selection is brought about, it is not done at the periphery. Oswald *et al.* (1960) were able to show differential responses in the EEG to certain patterns (their own names) in sleepers who did not wake. Moray (1969) was able to condition a GSR to a word using electric shock and to obtain the GSR when the word was presented in the rejected message without the listener being aware of it. Both these studies imply cortical analysis of signals of which the observer is not aware. But while relevant to selective listening, they are more concerned with the access to high levels of the brain by specific stimuli, rather than the selection or gating of incoming information along specific pathways. There are known to be efferent inhibitory fibres which run all the way to the cochlea itself, although their function is unknown. At every level of the auditory pathways efferent fibres end which take their origin from higher levels. Despite the fact that in some cases these efferent pathways have been observed to inhibit lower levels of the nervous system, their normal function is not understood. Galambos (1955), for example, found that stimulating the olivo-cochlear bundle inhibits the activy of neurons in the cochlea itself.

Wicklegren (1968) has recently published some very thoroughly controlled studies, which seem to show that no changes are found when attentional states change, except at the highest levels of the afferent pathway, namely the medial geniculate body and the cortex. Neither habituation, distraction, nor activities generated by the animal such as walking on a treadmill caused any reconizable changes at the levels of the auditory pathway below the level of the geniculate. On the other hand the changes at the geniculate and cortex were sufficiently reliable to be used as indices of the state of arousal of the animal. The changes were complex changes in the pattern of the evoked responses, not simple changes in amplitude. Thus the best evidence at present available suggests that control is exercised at those centres where more or less complex pattern discriminations are carried out (Neff and Diamond, 1958), and which receive inputs from both sides of the brain. Further analysis of specific local effects looks like being a very tricky job technically.

Some experiments have related EEG variables to attentional states. Wilkinson and Morlock (1965) and Wilkinson (1967) report changes in the EEG during reaction time experiments which may be attentional. And Walter (1964) has reported that with the presentation of repeated pairings of a flash followed by a click an 'expectancy wave' appears in the human EEG between the two stimuli, which extinguishes if the click ceases to follow the flash.

At present, however, it would seem most truthful to admit that all in all we know little of importance at the physiological level in connexion with selective listening. With other aspects of attention, especially arousal, quite a lot is known. But the problem of selection and rejection of individual speech messages is very difficult. The lack of progress cannot be laid only at the door of the neurophysiologists. After all, it is not for much more than a decade that attention has been much more than a rude word in the psychologist's vocabulary, and despite the real re-awakening of interest there is still so little agreement among the behavioural models proposed that it is too much to hope for substantial advances at the physiological level. What we need first are better behavioural experiments, using non-verbal signals which can be handled by physiologists. Somewhere in the brain there are changes from moment to moment in synapses, in excitation and inhibition in the execution of plans and their initiation and control. Recently a whole symposium was given over to the physiology of attention, and a good deal of agreement can be seen among the authors, especially about the origin of the alpha-rhythm (not basically concerned with attention), and the 'expectancy wave' (Evans and Mulholland, 1969).

# 7 The Nature of Selective Attention

Apart from the interest in selective attention which professional psychologists have shown, attention is so obvious a fact of everyday psychological life, so all-pervasive in the natural history of man, that one of the greatest problems for research is to limit the field. Gibson (1941) reviewed the concept of 'set' as then used in psychology and found that there were so many different uses of the word that in his opinion it had almost outlived its usefulness. When a concept becomes almost universally explanatory, it also becomes vacuous. (Although one should always remember that there are two theories which cannot be disproved, the vacuous and the correct.) There is no doubt that one of the reasons for the decline in interest in attention among psychologists during the decades preceeding the 1950s was the difficulty of behavioural definition. A definition was needed which would bring the phenomena of attention outside the skull into the domain of public observation, rather than allowing them to remain in the privacy of the mental life of the individual observer. In fact, several different uses of the word each have a valid claim to its use, but it is unlikely that they share a common mechanism.

Firstly, there is the use with which we have been concerned in this monograph, *selective attention*. By this is meant the ability of a listener, whether human or animal, to process only part of the information which he receives and to ignore the rest. This is what is measured *par excellence* in shadowing experiments. Secondly, degrees of attention may be mentioned in connexion with states of *arousal*. A drowsy observer is less capable of paying attention to the environment than an alert observer. Thirdly, there is 'mental concentration'. Wittenborn (1943) published two 'tests of attention' on the basis of a factor analysis of tests designed to measure attention in this sense. The two tests were heavily loaded with a factor, he claimed, which was independent of I.Q., vocabulary, etc., but strongly dependent on the ability to concentrate. The first of these tests presented groups of three digits at a rate of one per second, and after each group of three the listener was required to write a + on a score sheet if the first number of the three was the largest and the second the smallest, and also if the third was the largest and the first the smallest. The second test required the subject to listen to a list of letters, and after each one to write a + if it was a vowel following a consonant, a — if it was a consonant following a vowel, and a + if it was a letter immediately after either two consonants in succession or two vowels in succession.

Subjectively these tests certainly feel like tests of mental concentration, and performance on the two tests is highly correlated. However, performance on them does not correlate, for example, with performance on a shadowing task (Moray, 1969).

A fourth use of attention is to describe what happens in *vigilence* or *watch-keeping* tasks, which are characterized by the fact that the observer is not looking *at* something or listening *to* something, but rather *for* something, such as a faint auditory signal or a blip on a radar screen. *Search behaviour* might also be called attention, and has been investigated by Neisser (1967). And finally there is 'set', which despite Gibson's (1941) reservations is still alive and kicking, usually referring to a predisposition to perceive certain signals or make certain responses.

The above list is not exhaustive. It would be of great interest to have a systematic picture of which of these skills correlate with one another, for this might give us at least some indication of how many mechanisms are involved in 'attention'. It might well be, for example, that the relation between selective listening and arousal is such that arousal level acts as a parameter which will alter the over-all efficiency of selection and rejection as it varies. But no systematic investigation has so far been carried out.

We will therefore confine our theorizing to the problem of selective attention in hearing, in the sense of listening to one message and ignoring another. We have seen that a listener can obey instructions to select a message on the basis of its position in space, whether the voice is male or female, and whether it is louder or softer. To some extent it appears that the listener is using such physical characteristics to let him identify the message, after which (in the case of verbal messages) he uses the syntactic and semantic continuity of the message as a means of selecting it. When we claim that a person is in fact selecting a message, what are we claiming? What should our operational definition be?

Let us consider the case of two messages, consisting of passages of continuous prose, which are spoken by one voice and come from a particular position in space, perhaps the right ear of the listener. How can we show that he is able to select one and reject the other? And can we determine whether he can make use of the physical distinguishing characteristics for this purpose?

Let us begin by establishing the probability of reporting some particular signal from one of the messages in the absence of the other. Call this $p(1)$. Now do the same for the second message in the absence of the first, and call this $p(2)$. Now present both messages together. We will almost certainly find that the probability of reporting each falls. We do not initially tell the listener to choose one at the expense of the other. We simply present them both and ask him what he hears. We may now find that he reports a mixture of the two messages, such that

$$p\,(1)\mid(1+2) < p\,(1)\mid(1)\;\text{and}\;p\,(2)\mid(1+2) < p\,(2)\mid(2)$$

which should be read, 'the probability of giving response (1) when (1) and (2) are both presented is less than the probability of giving response (1) when only message (1) is presented', and so on.

This is not surprising, since presumably each message will mask the other. How do we show that the listener can select one and reject the other? Clearly by asking him to pay attention to one of them. Suppose that message (1) is slightly quieter than message (2), and we ask him to select the quieter one. We now run the experiment again, and if $p(1)|(1 + 2)$ is greater when he is trying to select (1) than when he is not told which to select, we have grounds for saying that he can select, and some of the initial reduction was due to distraction of his attention by the second message. If on the other hand there was no change, the reduction in performance is entirely due to masking and no selection is possible. The difference between the two-messages presentation, measured with and without instructions to select, is the effect of selectivity; while the difference between the selective mode and the original single channel case is the effect of masking. Obviously allowance must be made in the experimental design for shifts in criterion, guessing, etc. if the effect of attention is to be rigorously measured.

How might we distinguish between the selection of the message itself and selection on the basis of the physical characteristics which it has? It will be conceptually easier to consider the case of dichotic inputs to the two ears, although the same arguments and methods can be applied to two messages arriving through the same ear. Let us present message (1) through the right ear and message (2) through the left ear. We can go through the earlier stages to establish that attention does make a difference. We can then continue further, and compare the value of $p(1)|(1 + 2)$ under two sets of instructions, firstly to attend to the right ear, and secondly to attend to the message which is presented in the right ear. It is reasonable to suppose on the basis of the experimental evidence which has been collected over recent years that both instructions will show that the listener can select the message and reject the other. But now we change the position of the message (as Treisman, 1960, did in a shadowing experiment); we can now see how the probabilities of report vary with the switching of the message and thus quantitativley describe the listener's performance under the different instructions. The reduction in performance caused by switching the message when the listener is selecting on the basis of position will show the effect of the message as distractor, and the tendency to stay on the same ear when trying to follow the message will show the effect of the ear as distractor. These can be expressed best as the probabilities of performance contingent on a certain set of stimuli in a certain part of the listener's environment and contingent on a certain set of instructions. The effect of the instructions in altering the probability of correct response provides the measure of the effect of voluntarily paying attention, or voluntary auditory selectivity.

The opposite side of the coin has implicitly been described in the last paragraph, and is concerned with the involuntary switching of attention despite the efforts made by the listener to avoid it, and to listen to that which he has selected. An example is the transitory switch found by Treisman when the position of the messages change to opposite ears in dichotic shadowing. Again a provisional paradigm is fairly easy to describe. We will do so on the basis of loudness. Let us suppose that we have established the value of $p(1) | (1)$ and $p(2) | (2)$, and also both $p(1) | (1 + 2)$ and $p(2) | (1 + 2)$ when the listener has been given no instructions as to which message to select. Let us now suppose that message (2) is louder than message (1). We now ask the listener to select message (1), the quieter of the two, but observe that when he tries to do so $p(1) | (1 + 2)$ is actually *less* than $p(1) | (1 + 2)$ when he is not trying to select at all. We would then have to conclude that the activation of the selection mechanism results in the louder of the two messages capturing the attention, despite the attempt of the listener voluntarily to pay attention to the other. (It is not suggested that this outcome is probable, but it serves to illustrate the conceptual issues involved.)

Many other extensions of this analysis in terms of the relative probabilities of response in different conditions are possible. Moray (1969) has developed a notation for such analysis of attention. But the fundamental point is that there are in fact relatively straightforward ways of setting up operational definitions and experimental paradigms which will satisfy the most ardent paleo-behaviourist, even though they only give probabilistic statements. Basically we have to proceed by means of 'definition by exclusion'. It is necessary to rule out such things as masking, forgetting, frequency of use, etc., and only at the end claim that the observed effects are due to attention. The exact way in which the data are collected, whether as averages over runs, or signal by signal, will be critical to our understanding of what is happening. Treisman, for example has argued for an attenuation model, on the ground that the data suggest that the information in the rejected messages is less effective than that in the accepted message, but not completely excluded. But given scores which are percentages of words correct, partial success could arise not only from the partial attenuation of all the signals, but also by the complete blocking of some of them, or parts of all of them, which would be a Broadbentian model. Future work will probably need to use a much finer-grained analysis than has been used to date.

Let us move towards summarizing what is known about attention. From the experiments on shadowing it is clear that a listener *is* able to exercise considerable voluntary control over what he will hear. The criteria on which selection can be made include position, frequency spectra, loudness, and semantic continuity, and probably intersignal contingencies and rhythm. It further seems that just those features which may be used voluntarily are also those which may over-ride voluntary selection and cause switching. Thus when a signal is highly probable, it will be heard even when it is in the 'wrong' message, although if in the 'right' message it would normally help to keep attention directed to the latter. In addition there are certain signals which have a special role, such as those with a high emotional value for the listener, and some others such as translations into a language the listener knows well.

Earlier work seemed to imply that there was an almost complete blocking of the semantic content of a thoroughly rejected message, but this now seems to be incorrect. It was the partial loss of information which led Treisman to argue for attenuation rather than blocking of the rejected message. Again, shadowing work suggested that simple physical signals with no semantic content, such as pure tones, were not affected by selection, since listeners could report them from the rejected message. But this is now seen to be due to the relatively crude measures which were used to test the discrimination of the rejected message by listeners who were primarily concerned with the other message. Working with continuous speech it is almost impossible to analyse moment-to-moment performance: it is necessary to average over long runs of stimuli unless computer generated speech is available. But the experiments on the psychophysics of time sharing by Moray (1969, 1970a, 1970b), and the strong arguments put forward by Swets (1963) make it very doubtful if there is much difference between selection of verbal and selection of non-verbal signals.

This should encourage us to look for a unitary theory of auditory selection which will include both verbal and non-verbal signals. The writer's views on the direction in which such a solution lies are presented in greater detail in Moray (1969a). But the following outline will suggest how such a model might be constructed.

The argument for attenuation rests upon the assumption that if a message, normally received with 100 per cent accuracy, is received in some particular experiment with only 40 per cent accuracy, then the signals which comprise it have in some sense been 'attenuated' by 60 per cent. Now we should notice that what is actually recorded in such an experiment are 40 per cent totally correct responses, and 60 per cent incorrect responses, rather than all the signals being 40 per cent correct, taken signal by signal. The attenuation hypothesis concludes from the obtained data that *all* the signals are *partially* attenuated. But we could equally if not more plausibly argue that the data show that *some* of the signals are *completely* blocked. This is not to rule out the possibility of partial errors: one might, for example, argue that if the word 'chattel' were presented and the listener reported 'cattle' then there was 80 per cent or so correct report; Treisman and Geffen (1967) report such errors. But usually it is not on partially correct signals that the analysis is carried out.

To do justice to the attenuation hypothesis, one could interpret it to assert that, given a message where the signal-to-noise ratio has been lowered for all signals, nonetheless 40 per cent are still heard correctly, which is a perfectly legitimate assertion, although one would certainly expect such a model to produce a very large number of partially correct reports from the rejected channel, a finding which has not been reported in the literature.

The alternative, that some of the signals are completely blocked, or that part of each signal is completely blocked, is not of course an original idea, but is Broadbent's suggestion. But whereas he envisaged switching times of the order of hundreds of milliseconds, and switching rates of the order of two or three cycles per second, we will here assume that switching time is extremely short and switching rate rather high, since there is no firm evidence to the contrary. Some hints about the model have already been given in earlier pages: here it will be developed far enough at least to show that there are plausible alternatives to Treisman's model other than the logically very similar model of Deutsch. Indeed, what is being proposed is a functional rather than a structural model, although the exact quantitative form cannot yet be completed.

We know that the brain is especially sensitive to change, but relatively insensitive to steady state inputs. In other words, it keeps a time average of recent inputs and detects departures from this, of whatever sign.

Suppose now that when a listener selects one message and rejects another, the latter is completely blocked above the level where the running average is computed, but that changes in that average are monitored continuously. There is no real objection to this on the grounds of unnecessary circuitry, since all that is required is a simple differentiating device followed by a threshold which if exceeded calls the switch for one sample. The onset of each word in the rejected message, or at least many of the words, will be sufficient to call the switch so that one sample will be taken, but immediately the voluntary setting of the switch will over-ride the command. If pure tone signals are used, with their extremely abrupt onsets, they will always call the switch. Suppose therefore that a few milliseconds of many signals from the rejected message are in fact monitored, what will be the result? The probability of being able to report semantic content will be very low, since only a small sample of each word will be taken, not enough to allow its identification. But many signals taken together will certainly give enough information for simple judgements of pitch, sex of speaker, etc., to be made. If two signals begin at exactly the same instant, then only one of them can be sampled, and as we saw in an earlier section, ANDs will be very difficult to detect. The special properties of certain signals such as a listener's name we might suppose to arise because of the lowered threshold for patterns which are similar to the first phonemes of the name. When such a pattern is observed, the duration of involuntary sampling increases, with the eventual recognition of the name. (Notice that in Moray's 1959 experiment only about 30 per cent of presentations of the listeners' names were heard. This raises some problems for Treisman's model. The present model simply observes that only 30 per cent of occasions were the words sufficiently asynchronous in onset for the start of the name to call the switch.) All the assumptions of such a model are readily testable in single channel operation by interrupting prose messages, or by applying values from classical psychophysics of auditory signals which allow precise predictions. A plausible alternative to attenuation is therefore available.

But that is not quite enough. The first part of this final section drew attention to the complexity of experiments on attention. I also implied that the time had come for a functionalist approach. At present the evidence is in favour of none of the models unequivocally. And a change in methodology seems indicated. At the back of all the models lies the concept of the limited capacity channel, first fully elaborated by Broadbent (1958). All of them concentrate on the selection of one from two or more inputs. But it seems probable that a more general theory will be needed. There is evidence that attention may be shared, or competed for, between input and output, or between outputs, just as it is among inputs. Thus Baddeley (1966) found that an output task, namely random number generation, was altered by a secondary card-sorting task; while Moray and Harrison (unpublished) found that on the contrary the secondary task was affected. Treisman (1964a) observed that asking for simultaneous translation decreased the rate of shadowing that was attainable at a given level of accuracy, suggesting that the extra, internal load reduced the capacity of the channel. This aspect of selection, that *any* operation, whether input, output, or transform competes for attention, is not readily included in the conventional models. Neither Broadbent's, Treisman's nor Deutsch's models can easily be modified to incorporate such factors, although Posner (1965) and Moray (1967) have outlined possibilities. At present we need much more data before trying to quantify the relations of input and output competition.

Over all, the evidence certainly warrants the conclusion that voluntary attention is a psychological and biological reality. There is a substantial body of experimental data, and selective listening research has progressed steadily during the last ten years. On the other hand, theory at present is lagging. It is not that we are short of theories; rather that they have been formulated for the most part at so imprecise a level that it has proved impossible to disprove any of them. We require greater precision in enunciating theories, and greater precision in our measurements in order to reduce the plethora of ideas with which we are at present overwhelmed. As things stand it is hard at present to make *detailed* rather than general predictions from any of the models, and hence eliminating the incorrect ones is impossible.

However, the models do provide a framework for generating further research, and there are grounds for optimism. With new and powerful mathematical techniques, new experimental designs, and above all with the level of interest in the field which shows no signs of flagging, we may confidently expect the emergence of powerful and indeed useful quantitative theory in the near future.

# References

BADDELEY, A. (1966), 'The capacity for generating information by randomization', *Quart. J. exp. Psychol.*, vol. 18, pp. 119–30.

BAKAN, P. (1967), *Attention*, Van Nostrand.

BROADBENT, D. (1952), 'Listening to one of two synchronous messages', *J. exp. Psychol.*, vol. 44, pp. 51–5.

BROADBENT, D. (1954), 'The role of auditory localization and attention in memory span', *J. exp. Psychol.*, vol. 47, pp. 191–6.

BROADBENT, D. (1955), 'A note on binaural fusion', *Quart. J. exp. Psychol.*, vol. 7, pp. 46–7.

BROADBENT, D. (1958), *Perception and Communication*, Pergamon.

BROADBENT, D., and GREGORY, M. (1961), 'On the recall of stimuli presented alternately to two sense organs', *Quart. J. exp. Psychol.*, vol. 13, pp. 103–10.

BROADBENT, D., and GREGORY, M. (1963), 'Division of attention and the decision theory of signal detection', *Proc. Roy. Soc. (B)*, vol. 158 pp. 222–31.

BROADBENT, D., and GREGORY, M. (1964), 'Stimulus set and response set: the alternation of attention', *Quart. J. exp. Psychol.*, vol. 16, pp. 309–18.

BROADBENT, D. (1971), *Decision and Stress*, Academic Press.

BRYDEN, M. (1962), 'Order of report in dichotic listening', *Canad. J. Psychol.*, vol. 16, pp. 291–9.

BRYDEN, M. (1964), 'The manipulation of strategies of report in dichotic listening', *Canad. J. Psychol.*, vol. 18, pp. 126–38.

CHERRY, C. (1953), 'Some experiments on the reception of speech with one and with two ears', *J. acoust. Soc. Am.*, vol. 25, pp. 975–9.

CHERRY, C., and TAYLOR, W. (1954), 'Some further experiments on the reception of speech with one and with two ears', *J. acoust. Soc. Am.*, vol. 26, pp. 554–9.

DAVIS, R., MORAY, N., and TREISMAN, A. (1961), 'Imitative responses and the rate of gain of information', *Quart. J. exp. Psychol.*, vol. 13, pp. 79–91.

DAY, R. (1967), 'Fusion in dichotic listening', *Paper to the Psychonomic Society*, Chicago.

DEUTCH, J. (1960), *The Structural Basis of Behaviour*, Chicago U.P.

DEUTSCH, J., and DEUTSCH, D. (1963), 'Attention: some theoretical considerations', *Psychol. Rev.*, vol. 70, pp. 80–90.

DEUTSCH, J., and DEUTSCH, D. (1967), 'Comments on "Selective attention: stimulus or response?"' *Quart. J. exp. Psychol.*, vol. 19, pp. 362–8.

EGAN, J., CARTERETTE, E., and THWING, E. (1954), 'Some factors affecting multichannel listening', *J. acoust. Soc. Am.*, vol. 26, pp. 774–82.

EGETH, H. (1967), 'Selective attention', *Psychol. Bull.*, vol. 67, pp. 41–57.

EVANS, C. R., and MULHOLLAND, T. B. (1969), *Attention and Neurophysiology*, Butterworth.

GALAMBOS, R. (1955), 'Suppression of the auditory nerve activity by stimulation of efferent fibres to the cochlea', *Fed. Proc.*, vol. 14, p. 53.

GIBSON, J. (1941), 'A critical review of the concept of set in contemporary psychology', *Psychol. Bull.*, vol. 38, pp. 781–817.

GRAY, G., and WEDDERBURN, A. (1960), 'Grouping strategies with simultaneous stimuli', *Quart. J. exp. Psychol.*, vol. 12, pp. 180–85.

HERNÁNDEZ-PEÓN, R. (1966), in RUSSELL, R. (ed.), *Frontiers in Physiological Psychology*, Academic Press, vol. 1, pp. 121–48.

HORN, G. (1965), 'Physiological and psychological aspects of selective attention', in LEHRMANN, D. F., *et al.* (eds.), *Advances in the Study of Behaviour*, Academic Press, vol. 1, pp. 155–217.

HOWARTH, I., and ELLIS, K. (1961), 'The relative intelligibility threshold for one's own and other people's names', *Quart. J. exp. Psychol.*, vol. 13, pp. 236–40.

HUGGINS, A. (1964), 'Distortion of temporal patterns of speech: interruption and alternations', *J. acoust. Soc. Am.*, vol. 36, pp. 1055–65.

INGLIS, J. (1960), 'Dichotic stimulation and memory disorder', *Nature*, vol. 186, pp. 181–2.

INGLIS, J. (1961), 'Successive responses to simultaneous stimulation in elderly patients with memory disorder', *J. abnorm. soc. Psychol.*, vol. 62, pp. 709–12.

KIMURA, D. (1961a), 'Cerebral dominance and the perception of verbal stimuli', *Canad. J. Psychol.*, vol. 15, pp. 166–71.

KIMURA, D. (1961b), 'Some effects of temporal lobe damage on auditory perceptions', *Canad. J. Psychol.*, vol. 15, pp. 156–65.

KIMURA, D. (1964), 'Left–right differences in the perception of melodies', *Quart. J. exp. Psychol.*, vol. 16, pp. 355–9.

KOLERS, P. (1968), 'Bilingualism and information processing', *Sci. Amer.*, vol. 218, pp. 78–90.

KRISTOFFERSON, A. (1967a), 'Attention and psychophysical time', in SANDERS, A. (ed.), *Attention and Performance*, North-Holland, pp. 93–101.

KRISTOFFERSON, A. (1967b), 'Successive discrimination as a two-state quantal process', *Science*, vol. 158, pp. 1337–40.

LAWSON, E. (1966), 'Decisions concerning the rejected channel', *Quart. J. exp. Psychol.*, vol. 18, pp. 260–65.

MACKINTOSH, N. (1964), 'Overtraining and transfer within and between dimensions in the rat', *J. exp. Psychol.*, vol. 16, pp. 250–56.

MORAY, N. (1958), 'The effect of the relative intensities of message in dichotic shadowing', *Lang. Speech.*, vol. 1, pp. 110–13.

MORAY, N. (1959), 'Attention in dichotic listening: affective cues and the influence of instructions', *Quart. J. exp. Psychol.*, vol. 9, pp. 56–60.

MORAY, N. (1960), 'Broadbent's filter theory: postulate H and the problem of switching time', *Quart. J. exp. Psychol.*, vol. 12, pp. 214–21.

MORAY, N. (1961), 'Perceptual defence and filter theory', *Nature*, vol. 191, p. 940.

MORAY, N. (1967), 'Where is capacity limited? A survey and a model', in SANDERS, A. (ed.), *Attention and Performance*, North-Holland, pp. 84–93.

MORAY, N. (1969), *Attention: Selective Processes in Vision and Hearing*, Hutchinson.

MORAY, N. (1970a), 'Introductory experiments in auditory tone sharing: detection of intensity and frequency increments', *J. acoust. Soc. Am.*, vol. 47, pp. 1071–3.

MORAY, N. (1970b), 'Time sharing in auditory perception: the effect of stimulus duration', *J. acoust Soc. Am.*, vol. 47, pp. 660–61.

MORAY, N. (1972), *Attention and Performance IV*, North Holland.

MORAY, N., and BARNETT, T. (1965), 'Stimulus presentation and methods of scoring in short-term memory experiments', *Acta Psychol.*, vol. 24, pp. 253–63.

MORAY, N., BATES, A., and BARNETT, T. (1965), 'Experiments on the four-eared man', *J. acoust. Soc. Am.*, vol. 38, pp. 196–201.

MORAY, N., and FEE, M. (1969), 'The perception of pure tones in selective listenings' (in preparation).

MORAY, N., and JORDAN, A. (1966), 'Practice and compatibility in two-channel short term memory', *Psychon. Sci.*, vol. 4, (12).

MORAY, N., and O'BRIEN, T. (1967), 'Signal detection theory applied to selective listening', *J. acoust. Soc. Am.*, vol. 42, pp. 765–72.

MORAY, N., and REID, A. (1967), 'Two-channel immediate memory span', *Psychon. Sci.*, vol. 8 (6), pp. 249–50.

MORAY, N., and TAYLOR, A. (1958), 'The effect of redundancy on shadowing one of two dichotic messages', *Lang. Speech.*, vol. 1, pp. 102–9.

MOWBRAY, G. (1964), 'Perception and retention of verbal information presented during auditory shadowing', *J. acoust. Soc. Am.*, vol. 36, pp. 1459–65.

NEFF, W., and DIAMOND, I. (1958), 'The neural basis of auditory discrimination', in HARLOW, H., and WOOLSEY, C. (eds.), *Biological and Biochemical Bases of Behaviour*, Wisconsin U.P., pp. 101–27.

NEISSER, U. (1967), *Cognitive Psychology*, Appleton-Century-Crofts.

NORMAN, D. (1968), 'Towards a theory of memory and attention', *Psychol. Rev.*, vol. 75, pp. 522–36.

NORMAN, D. (1969a), 'Memory while shadowing', *Quart. J. exp. Psychol.*, vol. 21, pp. 85–94.

NORMAN, D. (1969b), *Memory and Attention*, Wiley.

OSWALD, I., TAYLOR, A., and TREISMAN, M. (1960, 'Discriminative responses to stimulation during human sleep', *Brain*, vol. 83, pp. 440–53.

POSNER, M. (1965), 'Effect of size and location of informational transforms upon short-term retention', *J. exp. Psychol.*, vol. 70, pp. 486–505.

REYNOLDS, D. (1964), 'Effects of double stimulation: temporary inhibition of response', *Psychol. Bull.*, vol. 62, pp. 335–47.

ROSENSWEIG, M., and WYERS, E. (1955), 'Binaural interaction at the inferior colliculi', *J. comp. physiol. Psychol.*, vol. 48, pp. 426–30.

SAMUELS, I. (1959), 'Reticular mechanisms and behaviour', *Psychol. Bull.*, vol. 56, pp. 1–25.

SAVIN, H. (1967), 'On the successive perception of simultaneous stimuli', *Percept. Psychophys.*, vol. 2 (10), pp. 479–82.

SCHUBERT, E., and PARKER, C. (1955), 'Additions to Cherry's findings on switching speech between the two ears', *J. acoust. Soc. Am.*, vol. 27, pp. 792–4.

SHAFFER, H., and HARDWICK, J. (1969), 'Monitoring simultaneous auditory |messages', *Percept. and Psychophys.*, vol. 6 (68), pp. 401–4.

SHANKWEILER, D., and STUDDART-KENNEDY, M. (1967), 'Identification of consonants and vowels presented to left and right ears', *Quart. J. exp. Psychol.*, vol. 19, pp. 59–64.

SHANNON, C., and WEAVER, W. (1949), *The Mathematical Theory of Communication*, Illinois U.P.

SHARPLESS, S., and JASPER, H. (1956), 'Habituation of the arousal reaction', *Brain*, vol. 79, pp. 655–80.

SPERLING, G. (1960), 'The information available in brief visual presentations', *Psychol. Monog.*, vol. 74, p. 11.

SPIETH, W., CURTIS, J., and WEBSTER, J. (1954), 'Responding to one of two simultaneous messages', *J. acoust. Soc. Am.*, vol. 26, pp. 391–6.

SUTHERLAND, N. (1964), 'The learning of discrimination by animals', *Endeavour*, vol. 23, pp. 148–54.

SWETS, J. A. (1963), 'Central factors in auditory frequency selectivity', *Psychol. Bull.*, vol. 60, pp. 429–40.

# 99 References

TAYLOR, M. (1967), 'Detectability theory and the interpretation of vigilance data', in Sanders, A. (ed.), *Attention and Performance*, North-Holland, pp. 390–99.

TEUBER, H.-L. (1962), 'Effects of brain wounds implicating right or left hemisphere in man; hemisphere differences and hemisphere interaction in vision, audition and somasthesis', in Mountcastle, V. (ed.), *Interhemispheric Relations and Cerebral Dominance*, Johns Hopkins.

TOLHURST, G., and PETERS, R. (1956), 'The effect of attenuating one channel of a dichotic circuit upon the reception of dual messages', *J. acoust. Soc. Am.*, vol. 28, pp. 602–5.

TREISMAN, A. (1960), 'Contextual cues in selective listening', *Quart. J. exp. Psychol.*, vol. 12, pp. 242–8.

TREISMAN, A. (1964a), 'Verbal cues, language, and meaning in attention', *Am. J. Psychol.*, vol. 77, pp. 206–14.

TREISMAN, A. (1964b), 'The effect of irrelevant material on the efficiency of selective listening', *Am. J. Psychol.*, vol. 77, pp. 533–46.

TREISMAN, A. (1964c), 'Selective attention in man', *Brit. med. Bull.*, vol. 20, pp. 12–16.

TREISMAN, A. (1967), '"Selective listening: Stimulus or response?" A reply', *Quart. J. exp. Psychol.*, vol. 19, pp. 362–8.

TREISMAN, A. (1970), 'Perception and recall of simultaneous speech stimuli', in Sanders, A. (ed.), *Attention and Performance III*, North Holland.

TREISMAN, A. (1971), 'Shifting attention between the ears', *Quart. J. exp. Psychol.*, vol. 23, pp. 157–68.

TREISMAN, A., and GEFFEN, G. (1967), 'Selective attention: perception or response?' *Quart. J. exp. Psychol.*, vol. 19, pp. 1–18.

TREISMAN, A., and GEFFEN, G. (1968), 'Selective attention and cerebral dominance in perceiving and responding to speech messages', *Quart. J. exp. Psychol.*, vol. 20, pp. 139–51.

TREISMAN, A., and RILEY, J. G. (1969), 'Is selective attention selective perception or selective response: a further test', *J. exp. Psychol.*, vol. 79, pp. 27–34.

VORONIN, L., and SOKOLOV, E. (1960), 'Cortical mechanism of the orienting reflex and its relation to the conditioned reflex', *Electroenceph. clin. Neurophysiol.*, Suppl. 13, pp. 335–46.

WALTER, G. (1964), 'The convergence and interaction of visual, auditory, and tactile responses in human non-specific cortex', *Ann. N.Y. Acad. Sci.*, vol. 112, pp. 320–61.

WICKLEGREN, W. O. (1968), 'Effects of state of arousal on click evoked responses in cats', *J. Neurophysiol.*, vol. 31, pp. 757–69.

WICKLEGREN, W. O. (1968b), 'Effects of walking and flash stimulation on click evoked responses in cats', *J. Neurophysiol.*, vol. 31, pp. 769–77.

WICKLEGREN, W. O. (1968c), 'Effects of acoustic habituation on click evoked responses in cats', *J. Neurophysiol.*, vol. 31, pp. 777–85.

WILKINSON, R. (1967), 'Evoked response and reaction time', in SANDERS, A. (ed.), *Attention and Performance*, North-Holland, pp. 233–45.

WILKINSON, R., and MORLOCK, H. (1965), Abstract in *Bull. Brit. Psychol. Soc.*, vol. 19, p. 10a.

WITTENBORN, J. (1943), 'Factorial equations for tests of attention', *Psychometrika*, vol. 8, pp. 19–35.

WORDEN, F. (1967), 'Attention and auditory electrophysiology', in SPRAGUE, J., and STELLAR, E. (eds.), *Progress in Physiological Psychology*, Academic Press, vol. 1, pp. 45–117.

UNDERWOOD, G. (1971), 'Shadowing and monitoring for selective attention', *Quart. J. exp. Psychol.*, vol. 23, no. 3.

YNTEMA, D., and TRASK, F. (1963), 'Recall as a search process', *J. verb. Learn. verb. Behav.*, vol. 2, pp. 65–74.

ZWISLOCKI, J. (1953), 'Acoustic attenuation between the ears', *J acoust. Soc. Am.*, vol. 25, pp. 743–52.

# Index

# Penguin Science of Behaviour

# Introducing Psychology

D. S. Wright, Ann Taylor, D. R. Davies, W. Sluckin,
S. G. M. Lee and J. T. Reason

*Introducing psychology* was specially commissioned by Penguin
Education from some of the staff of the Department of
Psychology at the University of Leicester; their collaboration
provides a wide range of specialist views within the coherence of a
common framework and a consistent style.

'*Introducing psychology* deserves a special welcome. It is well
organized, sensibly illustrated, clearly written and properly
documented; at the price it will be found more than competitive
for comparable American texts. The sequence of chapter is
sensible, going from structure and behaviour through the use of
experience, to symbolic behaviour, individual differences and
social influence.'
H. J. Eysenck in *New Scientist*

# Behaviour Therapy in Clinical Therapy
Victor Meyer and Edward S. Chesser

This text should be of interest to those already engaged in clinical
practice or research and those undergoing training who may
choose to enter this field. It should therefore be of value to those
training or practising in clinical psychology, psychiatry,
psychiatric social work and occupational therapy.

'This concise and readable book fills a long-felt need.'
*Lancet*

Victor Meyer is Reader in Clinical Psychology, Academic
Department of Psychiatry, Middlesex Hospital Medical School.

Edward S. Chesser is Nuffield Fellow and Honorary Lecturer in
Psychiatry, Middlesex Hospital Medical School.